Shifting Perspectives

TRIM YOUR WAY TO ONE-OF-A-KIND QUILTS

   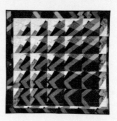

LORRAINE TORRENCE

C&T PUBLISHING

Text © 2006 Lorraine Torrence

Artwork © 2006 C&T Publishing, Inc.

Publisher: Amy Marson

Editorial Director: Gailen Runge

Acquisitions Editor: Jan Grigsby

Editor: Lynn Koolish

Technical Editors: Ellen Pahl and Susan Nelsen

Copyeditor/Proofreader: Wordfirm, Inc.

Cover Designer: Christina D. Jarumay

Design Director/Book Designer: Christina D. Jarumay

Illustrator: Richard Sheppard

Production Assistants: Zinnia Heinzmann and Kirstie Pettersen

Photography: Luke Mulks

Published by C&T Publishing, Inc., P.O. Box 1456, Lafayette, CA 94549

Library of Congress Cataloging-in-Publication Data

Torrence, Lorraine

  Shifting perspectives : trim your way to one-of-a-kind quilts / Lorraine

Torrence.

      p. cm.

  Includes index.

  ISBN-13: 978-1-57120-337-3 (paper trade)

  ISBN-10: 1-57120-337-0 (paper trade)

  1. Quilting–Patterns. 2. Patchwork. I. Title.

TT835.T665 2006

746.46–dc22

          2005029328

Printed in China

10 9 8 7 6 5 4 3 2 1

DEDICATION

To Augustin Fresnel,

without whose wonderful invention,

the Fresnel lens, the Multi-View lens

would never have appeared for use

in the quilt arena and this book

would never have been conceived.

ACKNOWLEDGMENTS

Lavish thanks go to all my students over the past 30 years for pushing me to figure out what I was doing and how to express it!

To my faithful and talented friends Diane Roubal, Gretchen Engle, and Cindy Hayes, who are always there when I need them, thank you is not enough.

For stepping in at the last minute to help me quilt the last quilts for this book, I am so grateful to Jennifer Pielow, Kate Sullivan, and Lisa Taylor.

Thanks to the terrific C&T staff, in particular Lynn Koolish, who liked this idea and supported me in realizing it.

Last but not least, special thanks to my husband, Mike, for always backing me up with humor and generosity.

CONTENTS

Thunderclouds Approaching, 56″ × 56″, designed by Lorraine Torrence, pieced by Lorraine Torrence and Cory Volkert, quilted by Jennifer Pielow, 2005

Repeated block quilts are familiar territory for most quilters. This book presents a different way to use repeated blocks. You make a set of oversized blocks and then trim them so that smaller blocks are cut from the originals, but with each cut, the blocks are trimmed in a different place. Sew them together to produce a unique shifted-image quilt that takes the repeated block quilt on a whole new adventure. Even better, you won't waste the trimmed-off parts—use them for a border that balances and unifies the quilt!

Here's an example of the concept, based on the familiar Nine-Patch block. I've tilted the original Nine-Patch block to make the quilt more interesting.

Tilted Nine-Patch block

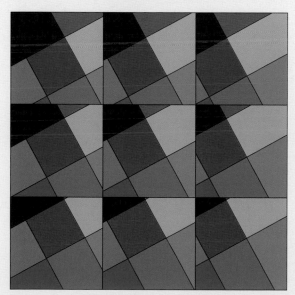

Shifted-image Nine-Patch quilt

The idea for this kind of quilt was sparked by the use of the Fresnel lens, also known as the Fly's Eye lens or the Multi-View lens. The lens multiplies the image seen through it into many small blocks, each of which is shifted slightly. This book will guide you through all the steps to make a dynamic Multi-View quilt, using a block pattern from the book or using a block of your own design. You

will also find many variations on this approach, including the use of other traditional blocks, rectangular blocks, and square blocks made into a rectangular quilt.

Collect these tools and supplies before you begin to make a Multi-View Image quilt:

- Multi-View lens (found at the back of this book)
- Square cutting ruler: 15″ × 15″ or larger
- Cutting ruler: 6″ × 24″ recommended
- Freezer paper
- Removable ½″-wide painter's tape (available at hardware and paint stores) or ½″-wide drafting tape (available at art supply or engineering supply stores)
- ¼″-wide quilter's masking tape (available at quilt shops)
- Plain paper, white or brown, 18″ wide or wider (butcher paper, kraft paper, shelf paper, or similar paper)
- Pencil
- Fine black marking pen

This book will teach you how to use the Multi-View lens to look at everyday items around you and find inspiration for original block designs. You will learn how to simplify those designs into easy-to-sew patterns. The book presents techniques for enlarging a design; cutting your block pieces using rotary cutting tools, templates, or tape on your rotary cutting ruler as a reference; and piecing blocks using partial seams for easy construction.

Instructions for four quilts are included to get you started and guide you through the concepts presented here. Each uses different cutting techniques so you can try them all out. Pick your own level: Easiest, Easy, Intermediate, or Advanced. Or strike out on your own and design an original Multi-View Image quilt yourself, beginning with Design Your Block starting on page 8. Design guidance in that chapter will help you in auditioning fabric choices while considering value, scale, and color—all are important ingredients in achieving balanced, unified quilts.

As always, there are many **right ways** to do everything! You may find shortcuts or better approaches, or simply use these ideas as a springboard to your own technique.

Let's get going!

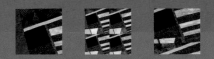

THE MULTI-VIEW LENS

Around 1990, this interesting tool appeared in many quilt shops throughout the country. It is a clear plastic sheet divided into 25 etched squares that show repeated images of a scene viewed through the lens.

The Multi-View lens

The formal name for this type of lens is the Fresnel (pronounced Fray-nell) lens. Other names—such as the Multi-View lens and the Fly's Eye—were given to the lens for novelty merchandising purposes.

The Fresnel lens was invented in France in 1822 by Augustin Fresnel and was used to amplify the light source in a lighthouse. The novelty version of the Fresnel lens, with 25 squares repeating the image, was adopted by the quilt world as a tool for viewing a quilt block to see what it would look like as a repeated unit in a quilt.

The fallacy was that the image in the upper left corner square of the lens was different from the one in the lower right corner. All the squares in between were each slightly shifted until the image in the opposite corner was a great deal different from the first. Since the shifting image distorted the view of the block repeated to make a quilt, the future of the lens as a tool marketable to quilters was short-lived.

The patterns of repeated, shifting images seen through the lens, however, were fascinating to most people, and I was no exception. Just as kaleidoscopes and teleidoscopes (devices that are like kaleidoscopes but contain lenses rather than mirrors) capture your imagination, the images seen through the Multi-View lens are equally engaging as repeated abstractions of the world around you. This design inspiration, in itself, seemed to me a good use of the lens for quilters. The other idea the lens gave me was that of emulating the shifting of the image that I saw when looking through it. **I realized that I could find a design I liked as I looked through the lens, distill the design into a simple, original quilt block, and make as many blocks as I needed for my quilt. I could then methodically trim each of the blocks into smaller blocks, providing the shift I saw through the lens.**

Turning the lens diagonally provided an even greater variety of design possibilities and, as I soon discovered, had distinct design advantages. We'll talk about that in the next chapter.

A scene using everyday objects

Spend some time looking through the lens. Look around indoors. Look at colored photographs in magazines. Take the lens outdoors. Hold it straight, hold it diagonally at different angles, and move it around to see if you can find designs you like as shifted repeats. These designs can be springboards to wonderful quilts that are as simple or as challenging as you want to make them. If you're ready to take the plunge and design your own block, read on. If you'd like to make one of the quilts in the book first, review Make Your Blocks, beginning on page 15, and choose one of the projects starting on page 34.

Same scene through the lens held straight

Same scene through the lens held diagonally

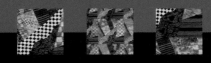

DESIGN YOUR BLOCK

Find a Design With Your Lens

As you look around through your lens, you will find many images ready to be interpreted in fabric as a wonderful quilt. Through the Multi-View lens, these images are multiplied 25 times and you see them more as abstract designs with color, value, shape, line, and texture rather than as familiar things with names. Continue to look around through the lens—indoors, outdoors, at colored pictures in magazines, at people, at buildings, at landscapes—positioning the lens straight and turning it diagonally.

As you do this, you will no doubt find some repeated patterns and designs that you like more than others. As you find designs that you like particularly well—those you think would make dynamic quilt blocks—make simple line drawings of the patterns or designs you see through the lens. Make some of the drawings when holding the lens straight and others when holding it diagonally. Each time, draw only what you see through **one** of the squares in the lens. Don't worry about the details. Try to distill the images into simple straight lines. You are **abstracting** the scenes you are seeing through the lens. You can include curves if you like—just keep them gradual because you will be sewing them later.

Draw the design you see through the lens.

Simplify, Abstract, Stylize

Once you have a few simple drawings, put away the lens and focus only on your sketches. Pick a couple that you like and draw each of them again, simplifying the design even more. At this point, try to forget the original image and don't worry about trying to make the single-block designs into balanced compositions. Individually, the block design will not need to be balanced. That will be remedied by the repetition of the blocks and the design of the border. Resist the temptation to make the block design too complex. Simple is good. This block will be one small part of the quilt, not the whole thing.

Simplify drawing.

This block will show shift clearly when repeated and trimmed.

Design Tip: Repetition

Imagine the Radio City Music Hall Rockettes. One dancer performing a simple step or gesture is not very interesting. But a line of 40 of them all performing that simple gesture in unison is thrilling and dramatic. The same principle applies to your block design. A simple block design repeated many times will be compelling and exciting. A complex block design repeated many times may look confusing and busy. Remember the Rockettes!

Design Pointers

Continue to refine a selected design until it satisfies you. Keep in mind a few design considerations specific to this approach:

1. When you eventually trim your blocks, a visual shift will be more obvious if you design your block with opposite corners that are different from each other. This difference can be in the form of very light versus very dark; very small spaces versus big open empty spaces; or intense or rich color versus black, white, and/or gray. Making the opposite corners different from each other will help you see diminishing or expanding areas as your trimmed blocks march across your quilt; the shift will be more noticeable.

2. When you trim your blocks to achieve a shifted image, you will be trimming off 3″ or more from at least one of the sides of each block in at least two rows horizontally and two rows vertically. If there is a design detail within that space on the edge of the block, it will completely disappear at some point. Before you design something in that space, ask yourself whether it would be better to see that design detail as a diminishing shape (large, medium, small) or a detail that you see in some rows but not others (large, medium, **nothing**). If you want to retain at least a shred of the detail in any block, **the design detail must extend into the block at least ½″ farther than the greatest amount to be trimmed off.**

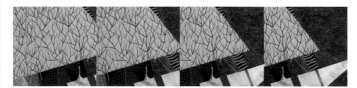

Yellow shape will successively diminish in size, but not disappear, as blocks are trimmed.

3. Note whether your block contains any vertical lines extending from the top of the block straight down to the bottom of the block. If you have kept your lens straight while looking for designs, this is possible. Or perhaps a horizontal line cuts all the way across the block from side to side. This will result in that vertical or horizontal line continuing straight through the entire quilt, regardless of the trimming you do. On the other hand, a block with lines running diagonally will give you lines that zigzag across the quilt, resulting in a more dynamic design.

Original block with straight seams

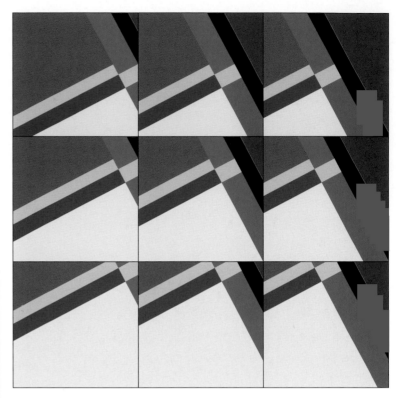

Shifted and trimmed blocks. Diagonal lines usually produce more dynamic designs.

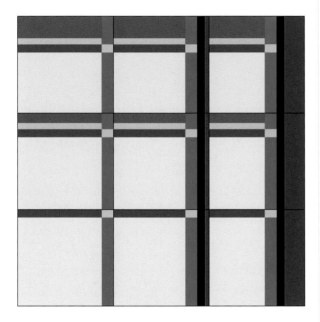

Shifted and trimmed blocks. Vertical or horizontal lines that connect in neighboring blocks may visually cut the quilt into strips.

Original block with diagonal seams

Block Size

The first time you make a Multi-View Image quilt, it may be easiest to stick to a simple format that is used in many of the quilts in this book: 9 blocks, each begun as a 15″ square and subsequently trimmed to a 12″ square. However, there are many variations that will allow you to make quilts with larger blocks, more of them, or even blocks designed as rectangles. See Variations on a Theme (pages 75–78) and the Appendix (pages 84–87) for more information on these different formats.

The size of the finished quilt will guide your decisions on how many blocks to make and how big to make them, keeping in mind that you will trim them. For example, if you want to make a quilt that will finish to around 40″ × 40″, you could accomplish that in several ways. Here are two possibilities.

■ Start with four 15″ blocks in each of 4 rows, each block trimmed to 9″ × 9″, sewn together with a finished 3″ border added all around. (8½″ × 4 = 34″; 34″ + 6″ = 40″)

■ Start with six 13½″ blocks in each of 6 rows, each trimmed to 6″ × 6″, sewn together with a finished 3½″ border added all around. (5½″ × 6 = 33″; 33″ + 7″ = 40″)

For more options, including quilts made from 16 and 25 blocks, see pages 27–29 in the Shifted Image chapter.

Make Your Master Cutting Guide

A final look at the design will help you evaluate the block and decide whether anything needs to change. Remember to do what the design needs, not what best depicts the original image you saw through the lens. That was just your inspiration—a starting point to a successful stylized image.

The **Master Cutting Guide** is your roadmap for making all the blocks. To make the Master Cutting Guide, draw the design onto a square of paper the size of your

blocks before trimming. As an example, let's use a 15″ × 15″ square original block. Draw around a 15″ square ruler on a large piece of paper. With a pencil, enlarge the final sketch you made to fill the 15″ square (see page 12 for instructions on enlarging a drawing).

Draw a line that is ½″ outside the 15″ square on all sides. This gives you a little extra insurance when stitching your block, and it serves as an indicator that a particular piece is on the edge of the block. When a piece is removed from the context of the complete drawing, this is not always obvious. After the ½″ is added, consider this to be part of the shape when measuring for cutting.

If there is an L shape or other irregular shape in your drawing, the addition of a seam will make the construction easier. Indicate that seam as a dashed line on the Master Cutting Guide.

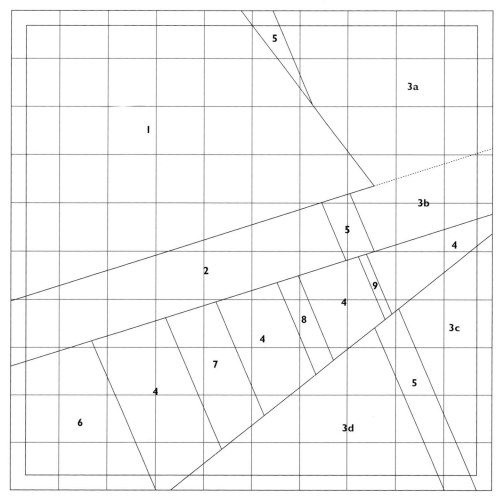

Master Cutting Guide

Enlarge a Drawing

To enlarge a sketch to a full-sized drawing, use one of the following methods:

- Look at the sketch and enlarge it freehand. This is straightforward and quick, but you may not get an exact enlarged duplication.

- Use an overhead projector to enlarge your drawing to the size you want.

- Take your drawing to a copy shop that does large-scale enlargements and can print on paper that is at least 15″ wide.

- Use the grid method. I find it to be easy—and I don't have to leave home. Divide each side of the small sketch into equal divisions and draw a grid. The greater the number of divisions, the more accurate your enlargement will be. Divide your larger square into the same grid. For example, if you divide your sketch into a 10 × 10 grid, do the same for your larger square. If your sketch is 5″ × 5″, your grid would be ½″. If your enlargement is 15″ × 15″, your grid would be 1½″. The key is to use the same number of equal divisions on the edge of the large square as you used on the small sketch. Replicate the lines within each small square of the sketch onto the corresponding square of the enlargement.

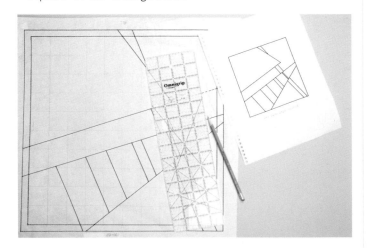

Fold fabric on drawing.

Refine Your Design

Before you finalize the lines on the Master Cutting Guide with permanent ink or marking pen, consider the dimensions of the pieces in your block. Round any odd measurements to the nearest ⅛″ so you can use your ruler for cutting as much as possible. For example, change a strip that is ⁷⁄₁₆″ in your design into a ½″ strip (⁸⁄₁₆″). The visual difference will be minimal, but cutting and sewing the blocks will be much easier.

Another final check of your Master Cutting Guide will allow you to see roughly how adjacent blocks will look when they touch each other. Roll your paper Master Cutting Guide into a tube and see where the lines on the left side of the square meet the lines on the right side of the square. Now roll the square so that the top of the design meets the bottom. After you do this, you may decide to change the angle or position of a line. Lines that come together, or nearly meet, may be harder to match or may look like a near miss.

Check where design meets from right to left.　**Check where design meets from top to bottom.**

After any adjustments are made, darken the final lines of your Master Cutting Guide with a black fine-point marking pen. This final, full-sized drawing will be your reference for the steps that follow.

Audition Fabric

Now it's time to choose the fabric for your blocks. You may choose to use the colors and visual textures of the scene that originally inspired you as you looked through the lens. Or you may exercise artistic license and forget about the original inspiration altogether. Do what works for the block—and ultimately the quilt.

As you pull possible fabric choices, remember that you will need the following:

■ A range in value (darks, mediums, and lights)

■ A variety of scale and print types (large, medium, and small prints; solids or near solids; stripes; checks; and so on)

■ Colors that work well together (Monochromatic and analogous color schemes may need something from the opposite side of the color wheel to enrich the color a bit.)

Make some tentative decisions about where each fabric should go. Remember that opposite corners of the block should contrast in some way so that the shift will be apparent (light in one corner, dark in the opposite; busy in one, plain in the opposite). Then make a practice block in one of the following ways:

■ Fold your fabric on top of the Master Cutting Guide so you distribute the fabric approximately as it will be positioned in the block. Mask the edges with white paper if needed. Even if some fabrics are not the ideal choice, you can use them in a specific position and then shop for different fabrics with the same color and value later.

Fold fabric on drawing.

■ Make reduced copies of your line drawing on white paper (8″ × 8″ is a good size) and color the areas with crayons or colored pencils to simulate fabric.

Color drawing.

■ Make two 8″ copies of your line drawing on white paper and cut one up to make paper templates. Use these to cut small pieces of each of your fabric choices and glue them into their spots on the other copy of the drawing.

Glue fabric on drawing.

- Use a drawing program on your computer to copy your line drawing and fill in the spaces with the colors, or even the visual textures, of your fabric choices. Print out the drawing on a color printer.

Final paste-up of full-sized block viewed through lens

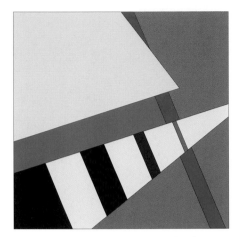

Use computer to generate and color design.

Look at your practice block through the Multi-View lens to see generally how it will repeat. This will give you a rough idea of how the block will look and alert you to any obvious pitfalls. For instance, you may see that the whole thing is too muddy and needs more contrast. Or perhaps what looked good as a single block is too busy as a repeated image. Maybe a selection of fabrics too similar in scale is making the quilt too confusing. Now is the time to correct any design features that are less than successful. After changes have been made, make a full-size test block by gluing final fabric pieces onto a copy of the Master Cutting Guide. Check again through the lens.

Avoid the temptation to make an intellectual decision about where fabrics should go in the block. Seeing it is the proof. People are often surprised when something they **thought** would look great looks not so great when they actually see it. The moral of the story is **make visual decisions visually!**

MAKE YOUR BLOCKS

Cut the Block Pieces

Block pieces can be cut in three basic ways:

- Rotary cutting

- Cutting with templates, including plastic, cardboard, and freezer paper

- Tape-on-the-Ruler rotary cutting

You may decide to use any or all of the methods in the same block, depending on the pieces you are cutting and your comfort level with each method. When measuring any parts of the block, always include the ½″ outer line in the measurements. Then add the seam allowances as instructed. To determine how much fabric you'll need for your blocks, see Calculating Yardage in the Appendix on page 83.

When you are designing your own block, I suggest that you cut enough pieces to make only one block to begin with. When the block is sewn together you will have a chance to look at it through the lens and double-check that you are satisfied with your fabric choices before you cut fabrics to make all the blocks for the quilt. You can also try out the different cutting techniques and see which will work best.

GRAINLINE

Regardless of the cutting method, cut all strips on the straight of grain, and make sure that the outside edges of the block are on the straight of grain whenever possible. In some cases, there is a visual reason to have a bias edge on the outside of the block.

Here are two reasons for placing the grainline in a different direction:

- A fabric with an obviously directional pattern needs to be oriented in a certain way that precludes putting the straight of grain along the outside edges of the block.

- Fabrics are scraps or odd shapes that are not big enough to cut in any direction other than off grain.

Of course, visual considerations often outweigh technical ones, and you can usually compensate in some way. For example, when the outside edge of the block, or parts of it, end up on the bias because you wanted a stripe to run diagonally in the block, stabilize the edge with a line of stay stitching, a strip of fusible interfacing, or water-soluble basting tape until you get the blocks sewn together.

ROTARY CUTTING

When the piece you want to cut is a strip, square, rectangle, or half-square triangle, you can cut it easily with a rotary cutter and a ruler.

To cut strips

Measure the width of the strips on your Master Cutting Guide and add ½″ to the width for seam allowances. If the strips are next to each other in the block, sew the strips together into strip sets and cut them as a unit.

Example: If you need strips that are 1½″ wide finished, cut strips that are 2″ wide × the width of the fabric.

To cut squares

Measure the sides of any squares on your Master Cutting Guide and add a ¼″ seam allowance on all sides. Any side of the square that falls on the edge of the block will have ½″ added instead of ¼″ for the seam allowance.*

Example: If you need a 2″ finished square in each of 16 blocks, each square needs to be cut 2½″ × 2½″. The quickest way to cut these squares is to cut a 2½″-wide strip across the width of the fabric (or the length, if a directional fabric demands it) and then cut the strip into 2½″ sections until you have cut your 16 squares. If the square falls on the edge of the block, you will actually be cutting rectangles 2½″ × 2¾″.*

To cut rectangles

Measure the sides of any rectangles on your Master Cutting Guide and add a ¼″ seam allowance on all sides. Any side of a piece that falls on the edge of the block should have ½″ added instead of ¼″ for the seam allowance.*

Example: A 2″ × 4″ finished rectangle would be cut 2½″ × 4½″. As above, you can quickly cut a 2½″-wide strip into 4½″ long segments.

***Note:** The extra ½″ around the outside of the block is to ensure that discrepancies in seam allowances within the block do not result in a finished block that is smaller than your intended size. It will give you enough extra to trim and square up the finished block to the size you need.

To cut half-square triangles

Half-square triangles can be cut from squares with a rotary cutter. To determine the size of the square, add ⅞″ to the finished short side (not the hypotenuse, or long side) of the triangle and cut a square that size. Then cut the square in half diagonally to yield 2 half-square triangles the size you want—the ¼″ seam allowance will be included. The hypotenuse, or long side of these half-square triangles, will be on the bias.

Example: For 2 triangles with finished sides of 3″, cut a square 3⅞″ × 3⅞″. Then cut the square in half diagonally once.

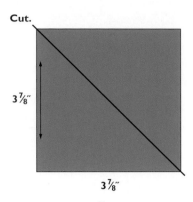

Cut triangles from a square ⅞″ bigger than the finished side.

To cut quarter-square triangles

If you want the long side of the triangle to be on the straight of grain, cut quarter-square triangles. This is important if the long side of the triangle is on the outer edge of the block; you want that edge on the straight of grain (see Example 2 below).

To determine the size of the square to cut, add 1¼″ to the finished length of the long side of the triangle, and cut a square that size. Then cut the square diagonally twice to yield 4 quarter-square triangles the size you want—the ¼″ seam allowance will be included, and the straight of grain will be on the long side.

Example 1: For triangles with finished long sides of 3″, cut a square 4¼″ × 4¼″. Cut the square in half diagonally twice.

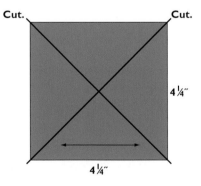

Cut triangles from a square 1¼″ bigger than finished side.

Example 2: If the long side of the triangle is on the outer edge of the block, measure the long side of the triangle on your Master Cutting Guide along the outer edge (the line you drew ½″ outside the block drawing); add 1¼″ to that measurement. Cut squares that size. Make 2 diagonal cuts in the square, **then** cut ¼″ off the side of the triangle that will be on the edge of the block.

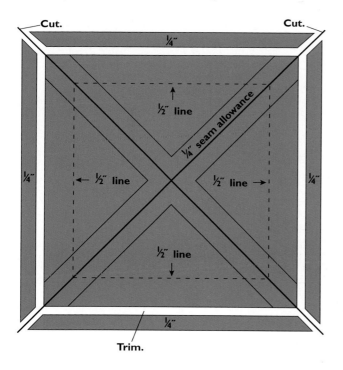

Cut triangles from a square 1¼″ bigger than the unfinished long side when the triangle is on the outer edge of the block. Trim off ¼″ from the outer edges.

CUTTING WITH TEMPLATES

You can make templates from cardboard, template plastic, or freezer paper. Be sure to trace accurately and cut precisely. Stitch the pieces carefully, using an exact ¼″ seam allowance, to ensure that your pieces will fit back together correctly.

Cardboard Templates

To make cardboard templates:

1. Duplicate your Master Cutting Guide on plain paper.

2. Cut apart the pieces along the lines.

3. Glue these pieces onto cereal-box or other similar-weight cardboard.

4. Add a ¼″ seam allowance to all inner sides of every piece. The outer ½″ will already be there.

5. Add any notations that will help you when cutting: which fabric, grainline, number of pieces to cut, pattern direction, top, bottom, and so on.

6. Cut out the templates on the outer lines.

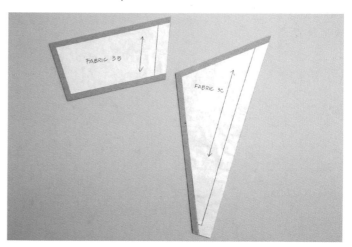

Cardboard templates

To use the cardboard templates:

1. Place the templates **face up on the right side of the fabric** or **face down on the wrong side of the fabric,** aligning the grainline arrows with the fabric grain.

2. Draw around them on a single layer of fabric.

3. Cut the fabric along the drawn lines.

Plastic Templates

To make plastic templates:

1. Trace each piece from the Master Cutting Guide onto template plastic.

2. Before you cut out the plastic template, add a ¼″ seam allowance to all inner sides.

3. Add any notations that will help you when cutting: which fabric, grainline, number of pieces to cut, pattern direction, and so on.

4. Cut out the templates on the outer lines.

To use the plastic templates:

1. Place the templates **face up on the right side of the fabric** or **face down on the wrong side of the fabric,** aligning the grainline arrows with the fabric grain.

2. Draw around them on a single layer of fabric.

3. Cut the fabric along the drawn lines.

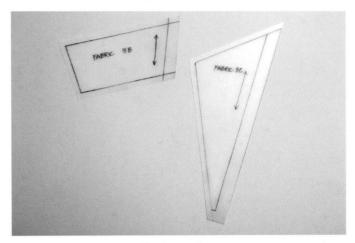

Plastic templates

Freezer-Paper Templates

I find freezer-paper templates to be very accurate because they are pressed to the fabric and do not move or shift when you draw or cut around them. Freezer-paper templates can be used several times. Simply peel off the freezer paper after you cut a shape and iron it onto the next piece of fabric to be cut. If the fabric you're cutting doesn't slide, you can cut more than one layer at a time with the freezer paper ironed to just the top layer.

To make freezer-paper templates:

1. Trace all the lines of the Master Cutting Guide, including the extra line ½" from the outside edge, onto the paper side (not the shiny plastic side) of the freezer paper.

2. Mark each area with important notations: fabric choice, grainline, how much seam allowance to add to each side, how many pieces to cut, and so on.

3. Cut the freezer paper apart on the lines.

To use the freezer-paper templates:

1. Iron a freezer-paper template onto the **right side** of the fabric, aligning the grainline arrows with the grain of the fabric.

2. Place the fabric with the ironed-on template on your cutting mat.

3. Place a ruler on one edge of the piece to which a ¼" seam allowance is to be added. Align the ¼" line of the ruler with the edge of the freezer paper template and cut.

4. Turn the ruler to the next edge to be cut, align the ¼" line with the edge of the freezer paper, and cut.

5. When you cut an edge to which ½" has been added, simply cut exactly along the edge of the freezer-paper template.

Remember to add seam allowances when using freezer-paper templates.

CUTTING WITH THE TAPE-ON-THE-RULER METHOD

This is one of my favorite methods for cutting pieces for Multi-View blocks because it doesn't use any formulas, measurements, or templates. Instead, you place tape on your cutting ruler according to the angles of the piece you want to cut. I find it more accurate than using templates, and it's especially good when you need to cut just a few irregular shapes.

Here's an example using piece 1 from the block shown in Design Your Block on page 11. I suggest you enlarge the block design to 15" using one of the techniques on page 12 so you can actually try out this technique. (See Tape-on-the-Ruler Cutting in the Appendix, pages 87–94, for instructions on how to cut the remaining pieces of the sample block.)

This is the cutting method used in the Easiest quilt project, starting on page 34.

Sample Block

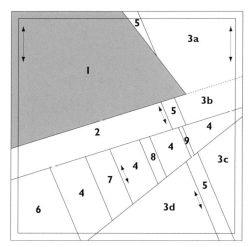

Master Cutting Guide with piece to be cut darkened

1. Mark the grainline on piece 1 on the Master Cutting Guide to make sure that the outer edges of the block will be on the straight of grain.

2. When cutting with tape on a ruler, you will first cut a strip of fabric as wide as the widest (or longest) part of the piece. Determine the width of the strip to be cut by measuring the longest vertical dimension of the piece.

In the example, measure the Master Cutting Guide from the line ½″ beyond the outer edge at the top to just over ¼″ below the longest part of the piece. This will allow for the seam allowance at the bottom edge of the piece. To measure this exactly, pencil in the ¼″ seam allowance beyond the bottom edge of the piece near the left side. In the example, the measurement is 9¾″. Cut a strip of fabric 9¾″ × the width of the fabric. You can cut the strip ¼″ wider for a little more leeway if desired.

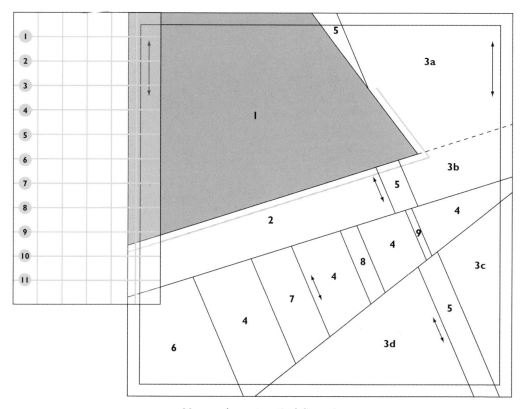

Measure longest vertical dimension.

3. Trim the selvage from the edge of the fabric at a 90° angle to the long cut edges, and you will have cut 2 sides of the piece already—the outside corner. The dashed lines in the illustration represent the edges that will be cut in the next steps.

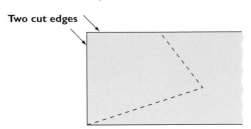

Trim selvage at 90° for outside corner.

4. Two sides of the piece remain to be cut. I've added letters to each corner of the piece to identify the sides. Now measure the length of piece 1 on the Master Cutting Guide, from the left outer line to point C, adding a ¼″ seam allowance on both of the remaining sides (B-C and C-D). This measurement is 12½″. You can add an extra ¼″ for a little more leeway. Cut a rectangle 12¾″ long from the strip.

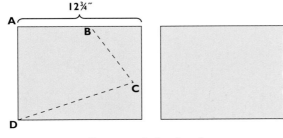

Cut rectangle for piece 1.

5. Look at your Master Cutting Guide. You can cut either of the 2 remaining sides next. I've chosen side B-C. Place the cutting edge of the ruler on the B-C line on the Master Cutting Guide. Now move the ruler to the right ¼″ for a seam allowance. The ¼″ line of the ruler should now be on top of the B-C line on the Master Cutting Guide. Now locate the upper left right-angle corner. This is the reference point you will mark with tape. Place ½″ removable drafting tape on your ruler on the outside edge of the block drawing so that the inside edge of the tape is aligned with the ½″ outer line. Draw arrows pointing to the inside edges of these 2 pieces of tape and write "CUT EDGE" on the tape. This is your **existing reference point**—

any seam or angle that has already been cut or sewn on the fabric you are about to cut.

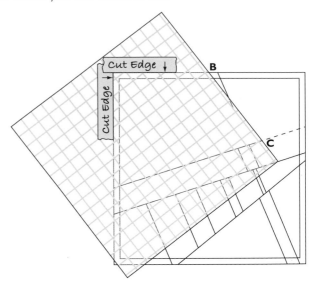

Place tape on ruler to mark reference point.

6. Place your ruler on your cutting mat, over the rectangle of fabric from Step 4. Align the inside right angle of the tape with the upper left corner of the fabric. Hold the ruler down firmly and cut the B-C edge.

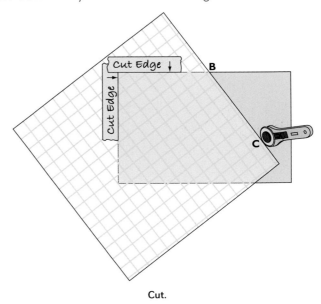

Cut.

7. Remove the tape from the ruler.

8. Refer to the illustration below and place your ruler along the C-D edge on the Master Cutting Guide. Slide the cutting edge of the ruler out beyond the C-D line so the ¼″ line of the ruler is on top of the C-D line on the Master Cutting Guide.

9. You now have the right angle at the upper left corner of the piece as well as the B–C line you just cut to use as reference points. Position 2 pieces of ½″ removable tape on the ruler at the outside corner of the Master Cutting Guide as you did before. Then add a piece of ¼″ quilter's masking tape along the outside of the B–C line of the Master Cutting Guide.

The reason I use ½″ removable tape in one place and ¼″ masking tape in the other is that the removable painter's or drafting tape will not leave a residue on your ruler and it's always preferable to masking tape. The ¼″ masking tape is more convenient on an inner seam because it accurately represents the seam allowance. Just be sure not to leave the ¼″ masking tape on your ruler longer than needed.

10. Draw an arrow pointing to the outside edge of the ¼″ masking tape and write "CUT EDGE" along that side of the tape.

11. Place the ruler on top of the partially cut piece of fabric on your cutting mat. Align the inside edges of the ½″ tape with the right-angle corner of the fabric and place the "CUT EDGE" side of the ¼″ masking tape along the cut B–C edge of the fabric. In the event that you cannot align both of these reference points exactly with the partially cut piece, the more important one to use is the ¼″ tape on the B–C line. This will ensure that the angle on the inside of the block is accurate. The extra ½″ added to the outside edge of the block is there in case of errors and for squaring up the block after it is sewn together. Now cut the C–D line.

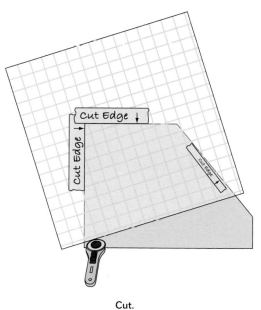

Cut.

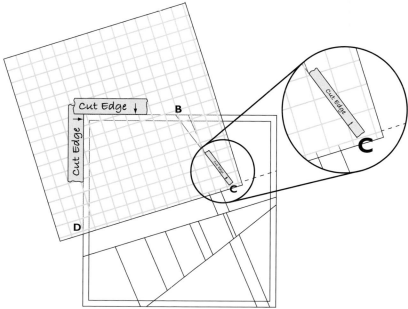

Place tape on ruler to mark reference points.

It is inevitable that at some point you will have found the perfect fabric for your blocks, only to discover later that you are a tiny bit short of having enough of the fabric to complete all the blocks.

If the fabric falls on the edge of your block, the good news is that you may be able to make all the blocks after all. Remember that you will be cutting some portion off of every edge of the block somewhere in the quilt. If you have enough of your fabric to cut every edge piece completely except one, and you are only a couple of inches short, use that one in a block where it will be trimmed off. It only means that you are committed to trimming the blocks and you won't have quite as much in trimmings for the border as you would have. Here's an example of a block I made when I ran short on one of the fabrics. If I hadn't told you, you would never have known!

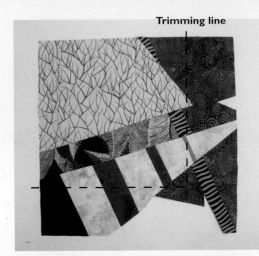

Trimming line

I positioned the block in the quilt so that the missing portion would have been cut off anyway during the trimming process.

Construct the Blocks

Especially when you are designing your own blocks, I suggest that you cut only enough pieces to sew 1 block together at first. This allows you to view 1 block through the lens and make sure you like the design and fabric choices before continuing. It also allows you to make sure that you're cutting out all the pieces correctly.

Sew together the cut parts of your block the same way most quilt blocks are sewn together: sew smaller pieces into rows or larger sections and then sew the rows or sections together. Always try to find a seamline that goes all the way across the block or block section you are sewing so that you are sewing straight lines and avoiding set-in seams if possible.

The sample block shown below can be sewn together as follows.

1. Sew 3a to 5; sew this unit to 1.

2. Sew 2, 5, and 3b to create a unit; sew this to the 1-5-3a piece. Press the seam open or toward 1.

3. Add the 6-4-7-4-8-4-9-4 section.

4. Lastly, sew 3d, 5, and 3c together to create a unit; add this unit to complete the block.

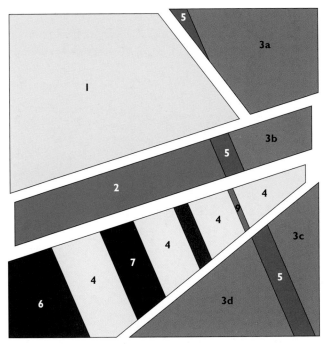

Sew block together in units.

Note that in this block, piece 5 appears to run through the block with 2 interruptions. The block design will be most effective if these seamlines are in a straight line. The alignment of these seams is worth taking care to do well. (See Special Lesson: Aligning Seams That Have No Reference Point, Part 1, on the next page, to learn how to do this.)

Aligning Seams That Have No Reference Point, Part 1

Proper alignment of seams is important in a block, such as the one shown, in which a strip appears to continue through a block but is interrupted by other pieces.

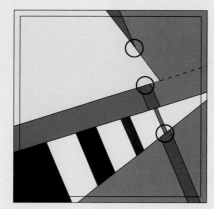

These seams must be aligned to their neighboring pieces in a specific way for the best effect.

If the seams in the turquoise and black wavy stripe (shown in blue in the illustration) are not aligned throughout the block, the illusion of the continuance of the strip behind the other parts of the quilt, and the illusion of depth, will be lost. It is easy to create and maintain this illusion using your ruler to mark an alignment point.

1. Construct each "row" of the block, but do not sew the rows together yet. Turn the 1–5–3a section over and place a ruler along the seamline between the turquoise and black stripe and the brown fabric. Make a mark at the bottom of the yellow piece where the seam would be if it continued.

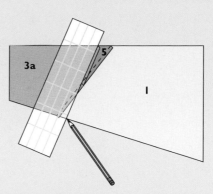

Mark seamline on back of 1–5–3a section.

2. Align the next row with this first row, matching the seamline of the turquoise and black fabric with the mark you just made. Pin and stitch the seam.

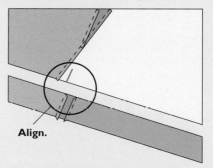

Align.

Align seam with pencil mark.

3. Repeat this procedure whenever seams need to **appear** as though they continue. On the wrong side of the fabric, align the ruler with the seam that needs to continue and mark the point where it would cross the next seamline if it did continue.

Marking the point where the interrupted seam would have fallen will make it easy to align the next seam, making it appear as a continuation of the same seam.

Preview the Blocks as a Quilt

When you have finished sewing your first block together, put it on your design wall or cutting table (uneven edges and all) and take a look at it through the Multi-View lens and evaluate your design. Does it repeat in an interesting way? Are the values varied enough? Do you like the color and scale? If you are dissatisfied, go back to the drawing board and change the things you don't like. If you do like the block, go ahead and make the rest of the blocks for your quilt.

Make Multiple Blocks

Repeat the process you used above for cutting all of the pieces for all the blocks. Make all the strip sets necessary for cutting the combination pieces. If you choose to cut with the Tape-on-the-Ruler method, you can use the first of each piece you cut as a template for the rest of the pieces, or you can assembly-line cut by making the same cut in all the same pieces while your tape is still positioned on the ruler.

When all the pieces are cut, stack them up in their proper relationship and sew them in the same order as you did for your first block. Sew the blocks in assembly-line fashion, sewing the same seam in all the blocks at the same time. Press the blocks so they are smooth and flat.

Square Up the Blocks

Use a 15″ (or larger) square cutting ruler to square up your blocks. Place the ruler on the Master Cutting Guide and mark a few prominent angles and seams with tape. You should only need 2 or 3 reference points. Mark the tape with the arrows and words that will tell you which side of the tape to use next to the seams. Remove the ruler from the Master Cutting Guide and place it on top of a fabric block on your cutting mat. Align the taped references with the fabric counterparts in the block and trim.

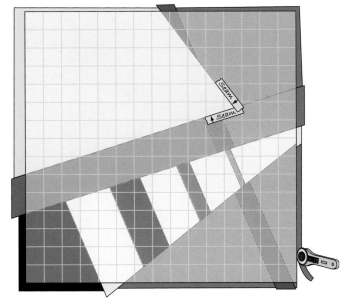

Square up block.

You may find that the tape does not line up perfectly with the seams in the block due to slight cutting or piecing variations. Don't worry about this too much. Just try to position the taped ruler the same way for each block. Trim around the ruler to cut the block to the size you want your original block to be. The goal is to make and cut blocks so they will be as close to identical as possible.

If you chose to make a 15″ original block, trim your block to 15″ square, not 15½″. It will finish at 14½″ × 14½″.

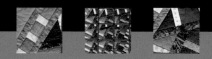

Looking at the block through the Multi-View lens gives you an idea of how it will look if it shifts as the blocks repeat through the set. It is easy to achieve this shift when you make blocks larger and then trim them to a smaller final block size. Each block is trimmed in a different, specific place.

Occasionally, trimming the blocks does not yield a design that is superior to the repeated full-size blocks. Or perhaps you will find an arrangement of the original full-sized blocks that is more dynamic than the shifted-image format. There is nothing wrong with departing from the original itinerary for your quilt trip if the new destination is more interesting. With this in mind, I suggest you always audition your blocks in several arrangements or settings before you trim them to create a shifted image. Look at the block arrangements I tried for the four different project quilts to see some of the possibilities (pages 42–43, 53, 64–65, and 74).

To simulate trimmed blocks, fold under the edges according to the trimming plans on pages 26–29 and place the blocks next to each other on your design wall. Take pictures of all the possibilities, both full size and folded, to see which you like best.

Remember: Make visual decisions visually; don't try to imagine what your blocks would look like in different arrangements.

Trim Blocks for a Shifted Image

If you decide you want to shift the image, place the blocks on your design wall and number them with a piece of masking tape, removable tape, or a label of some kind. Begin numbering in the upper left corner and number across each row from left to right.

See the diagrams that follow to determine how to trim your blocks. Trimming depends on the size and number of blocks. All the diagrams are based on square blocks that are trimmed to square blocks, resulting in a square quilt. See pages 84–85 to learn the formula for trimming any size and number of blocks to any finished size with any amount of shift. As a general guideline, you must trim at least 1½˝ to have a noticeable change from block to block. Variations for rectangular blocks or rectangular quilts made with square blocks are discussed in Variations on a Theme, starting on page 75. See the Appendix on pages 85–86 for using the formula with rectangular blocks. Once you are familiar with the methods, you can create your own trimming diagram.

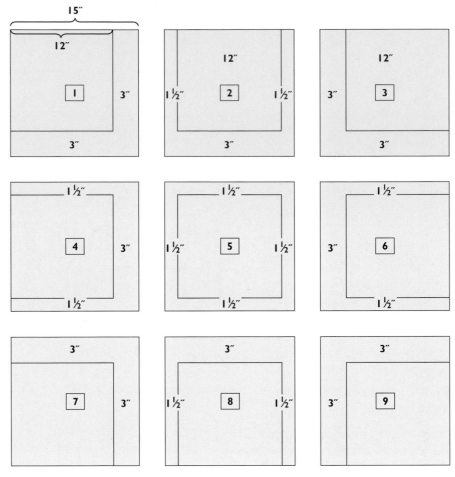

Nine 15″ blocks trimmed to 12″

As an example, let's trim 9 blocks using the 9-block diagram above to achieve a shifted image. The 9 blocks have all been squared up to exactly 15″ as shown on page 24 and are numbered on the design wall. Now you are ready to cut.

The difference between the size of the original 15″ block and the 12″ trimmed block is 3″. You will need to remove a total of 3″ from the width and the height of each block in some combination of cuts. The diagram shows that the block labeled 1 must have 3″ cut off the right side and 3″ cut off the bottom side to yield a 12″ block. Measure over 12″ from the left side of the block and make the cut, rather than measuring over 3″ from the right side of the block and making the cut. **The important thing is the measurement of what remains after you make the cut, not the measurement of what you trim off.**

1. Beginning with Block 1, position the 12″ lines on the ruler at the upper left corner of the block and trim around the other 2 corners of the cutting ruler to yield the 12″ square.

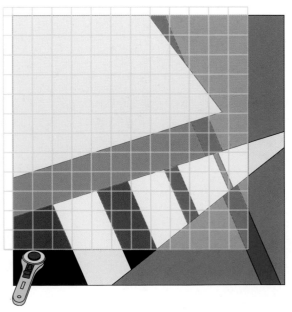

Block 1: Trim to 12″ x 12″ by cutting 3″ off bottom and right side.

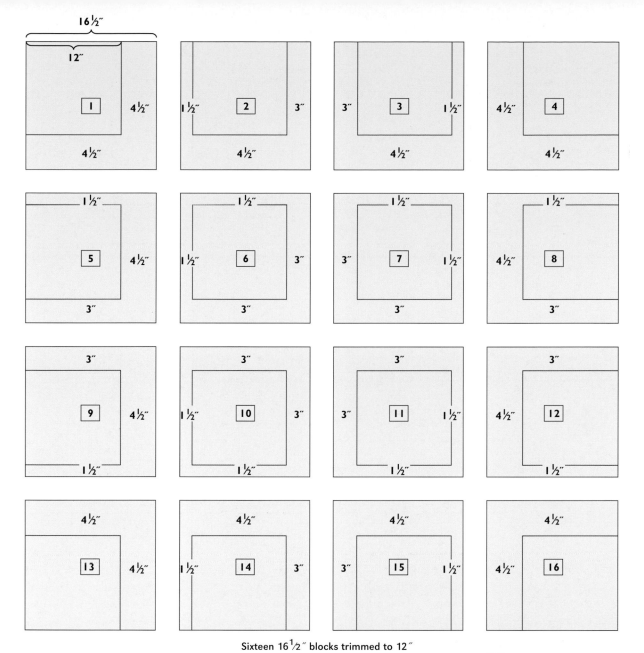

Sixteen 16 1/2″ blocks trimmed to 12″

2. Move on to Block 2 and look at the diagram to see the amount you need to trim from each side of the block. Note that the cut block position shifts 1½″ to the right in this block but remains at the top of the original block across the whole top row. Make a horizontal cut across the block that is 12″ down from the top of the large block. Now make a vertical cut 1½″ in from the left side of the block. After this cut is made, make another vertical cut 12″ from the new left edge of the block, to ensure the block will be exactly 12″ square.

3. Continue to cut the 15″ blocks down to 12″ blocks using the diagram as your guide. Remember to make 12″ cuts from an existing cut whenever possible. **Be sure to save all your trimmings. You can use them when you** design your border.

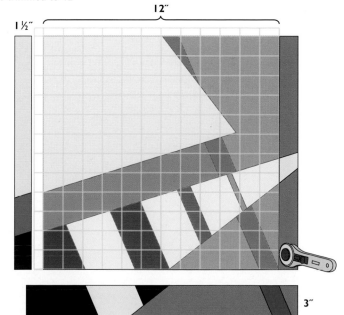

Block 2: Trim block to 12″ × 12″.

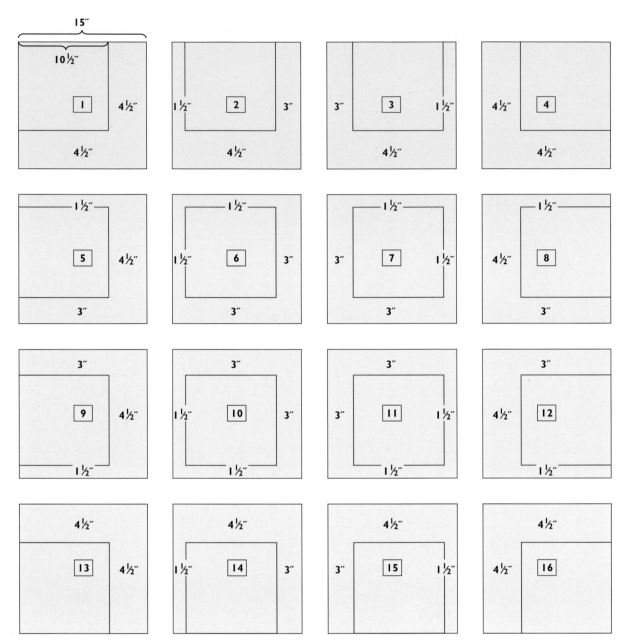

Sixteen 15″ blocks trimmed to 10$\frac{1}{2}$″

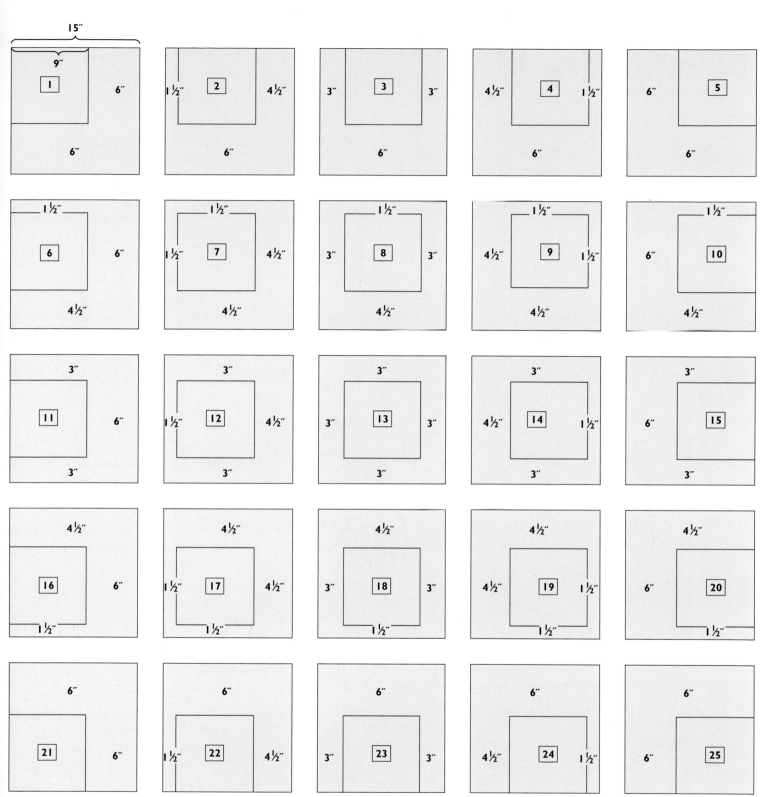

Twenty-five 15″ blocks trimmed to 9″

Do You Need Sashing?

When all the blocks are trimmed, place them edge to edge on your design wall in the numbered order. Occasionally, the shifted-image blocks will look busy or too close in value when set next to each other. A sashing strip between the blocks may remedy this.

Audition different colors and widths of strips with your blocks on the design wall. When you find a sashing fabric that you like, cut the strips as wide as the auditioned sashing **plus** ½″ for seam allowances. (See page 79 for Eileen Alber's *Marimeko Swatches* quilt with sashing.)

Sew the Blocks Together

For quilts without sashing, sew the blocks into rows. Press the seams in opposite directions from row to row. Sew the rows together, nesting the opposing seams to align the corners of the blocks perfectly.

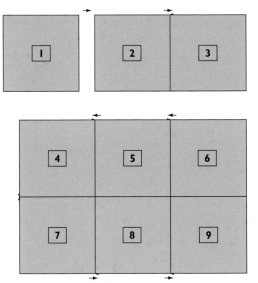

Sew blocks and rows together without sashing.

For quilts with sashing, sew the rows of blocks together with a sashing strip between each block. The sashing strips should be cut to the length of the blocks. Press the seams toward the sashing. Cut sashing strips to the length of the rows and sew the rows together with sashing between each row. Press the seams toward the sashing.

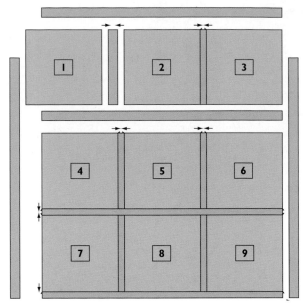

Sew blocks and rows together with sashing.

Another Option
You can add sashing corner squares to the horizontal sashing rows for a different look. Cut all the sashing strips to the length of the blocks and cut squares from a contrasting color.

Now your quilt is ready for the border!

BORDERS

You may have shuddered as you cut through your pieced blocks for the shifted image, but now you can put those trimmings to good use and feel better about cutting them off in the first place.

The best way to design the border is to audition many possibilities on your design wall. Put the pieced quilt top on your wall and analyze it. It probably changes in value and/or color from the upper left corner to the lower right corner. Or perhaps it has a busy pieced section in one corner and a simple plain one in the opposite corner. Does this shift need to be accentuated with more light in a light corner and more dark in a dark corner? Or maybe it would be better to contain a light corner with a dark border, place a busy border around a plain corner, or add a neutral corner around a brightly colored one.

You won't know without looking at the possibilities. Arrange the trimmings of your blocks (or just parts of them) around the quilt until you get a satisfying result. The overwhelming impulse is to use a trimming just as it is when you pick it up. But also consider cutting out the similar areas of several trimmings and piecing them together to make a border area of concentrated details.

Small pieces sewn together for border

You might also piece just a small section of the border with trimmings and then use unpieced fabric for the rest of the border. This might be exactly what the quilt needs to accent the blocks or to keep it from being too busy.

Partly pieced border mixed with plain fabric

One of my students made a fabulous Multi-View Image quilt in class, and after a year of trying to make a border from trimmings, she finally realized that the quilt didn't need the trimmings at all. It looked great with a simple 2″ black strip sewn around it as a border.

Other border options include the following:

- A narrow strip of fabric (audition for width) can be sewn around the inner quilt to create an inner border to separate it from a border of block trimmings. This is usually always preferable when you use sashing. Repeat the width and color of the sashing around the outside of the inner quilt before adding the border.

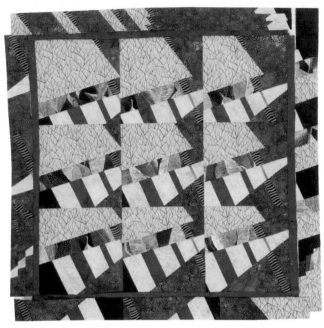

Narrow inner border

- The trimmings can be sewn directly onto the inner quilt and then finished with one or more plain border strips.

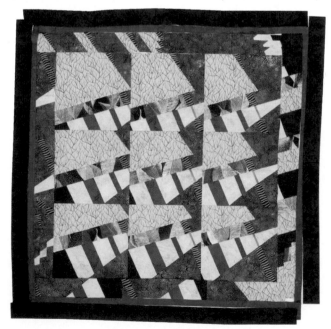

Pieced and plain borders

- A pieced border can be designed specifically for the quilt. Instead of using trimmings, you may decide that the quilt needs a border of several strips, or one that is diagonally pieced to echo piecing in the blocks.

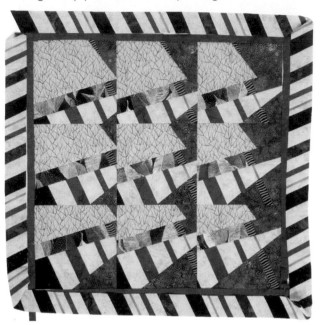

Pieced border

- A narrow inner border can be used with a plain border about half the width of the blocks.

Narrow inner border and plain outer border

■ The inner quilt can be placed on point with plain triangles sewn onto the corners to square it up. A pieced border of trimmings can be added to this.

On-point quilt with corner triangles and border of trimmings

If you piece together trimmings or parts of trimmings for your border, you may have to rip out parts that don't work, replace them with parts from another area, or make more of some parts using leftover fabric scraps.

Whatever you decide, keep in mind that the border should enhance the design of the inner quilt rather than eclipsing it or competing with it. The border should be a unifying factor and is not the place to introduce a new technique, a new color, or, usually, a new fabric. Once again, **make visual decisions visually!**

EASIEST BLOCK QUILT

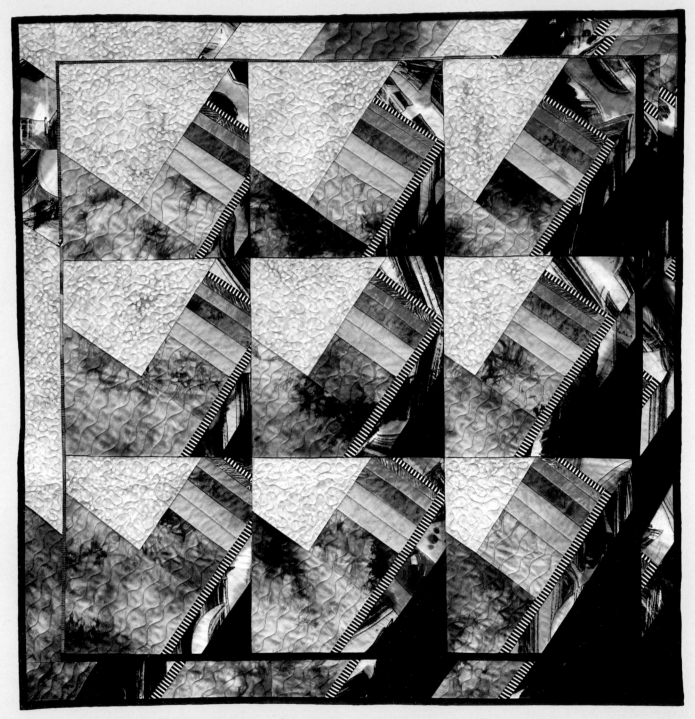

Shifted Napoleons, 38$\frac{1}{4}$″ × 38$\frac{3}{4}$″, by Lorraine Torrence, quilted by Gretchen Engle, 2005

Easiest Block

Here is a simple block design that is easy to sew, yet effective as a trimmed unit. Notice that the opposite corners are different from each other and that the block includes a range of values (darks, mediums, and lights) and varying scale (big areas, medium areas, and small areas). The diagonals create a more dynamic design than uninterrupted verticals and horizontals. Read more about these design pointers on page 47.

Cutting methods: For this quilt, you will use a combination of Tape-on-the-Ruler cutting (or templates, if you prefer) and strip piecing.

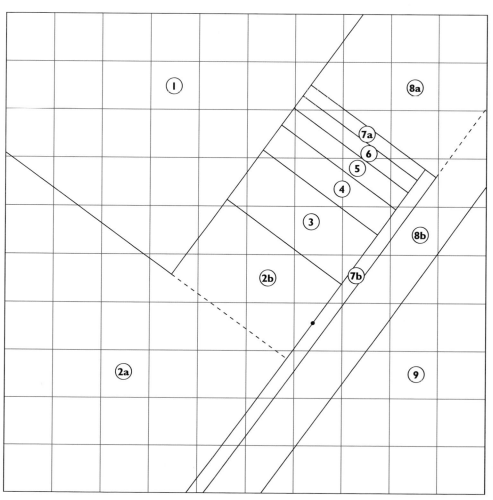

Block Diagram for Easiest Block (10 × 10 grid)

Fabric Requirements

Yardage is based on 42"-wide fabric.

Fabrics are listed by number, value, and the color used in the quilt shown.

See page 5 for other supplies you will need.

Fabric	9-Block Quilt	16-Block Quilt
Fabric 1 (light value, allover visual texture) Light blue-green batik	1 yard	$1\frac{1}{2}$ yards
Fabric 2 (medium-light value with more pattern than fabric 1) Mottled blue-green	1 yard	$1\frac{5}{8}$ yards
Fabric 3 (medium value, lightly textured) Khaki green	$\frac{1}{4}$ yard	$\frac{1}{4}$ yard
Fabric 4 (medium value, bright) Magenta	$\frac{1}{4}$ yard	$\frac{1}{4}$ yard
Fabric 5 (medium-light value, bright) Orange	$\frac{1}{4}$ yard	$\frac{1}{4}$ yard
Fabric 6 (medium-light value, bright) Orange print	$\frac{1}{4}$ yard	$\frac{1}{4}$ yard
Fabric 7 (high-contrast accent) Black-and-white stripe	$\frac{1}{4}$ yard	$\frac{3}{8}$ yard
Fabric 8 (large-scale print, high contrast) Green and purple dark print	$\frac{7}{8}$ yard	$1\frac{1}{4}$ yards
Fabric 9 (very dark solid or mottled fabric) Dark blue	$\frac{7}{8}$ yard	$1\frac{1}{8}$ yards
Backing*	$2\frac{3}{4}$ yards	$3\frac{3}{8}$ yards
Batting*	49" × 49"	60" × 60"
Binding*	$\frac{1}{2}$ yard	$\frac{1}{2}$ yard

*Backing, batting, and binding quantities are approximate, based on: 15" blocks trimmed to 12" and sewn together without sashing; 4" borders added on all sides.

Instructions

GETTING STARTED

1. Preshrink and iron your fabric.

2. Make a Master Cutting Guide following the instructions beginning on page 11. The block drawing on page 35 is divided into a grid of 10 divisions; transfer the design to a 15" square divided into a 10 × 10 grid of $1\frac{1}{2}$".

3. Remember to add a pencil line around the 15" square cutting guide, $\frac{1}{2}$" outside the perimeter of the square for extra insurance when squaring up blocks later.

4. Make a copy of your Master Cutting Guide and audition your fabric choices by cutting pieces and gluing them to the copy. Look at the mocked-up block through your Multi-View lens to see how it will repeat. This won't be an exact version of how it will look, but it will give you a good idea.

CUTTING

All cutting instructions include ¼″ seam allowances.

Cut strips across the width of the fabric (42″ wide) and set aside in numerical order. Cutting specific to the 16-block quilt is given within brackets [ ].

Fabric	Used for	Number and Size to Cut
Fabric 1	Piece 1	3 [4] strips, 10″ wide
Fabric 2	Strip set	2 strips, 3½″ wide
	Piece 2a	2 [4] strips, 10″ wide
Fabric 3	Strip set	2 strips, 2½″ wide
Fabric 4	Strip set	2 strips, 1½″ wide
Fabric 5	Strip set	2 strips, 1¼″ wide
Fabric 6	Strip set	2 strips, 1″ wide
Fabric 7	Strip set	2 strips, ⅞″ wide
	Piece 7b	9 [16] rectangles, 1″ × 14″
Fabric 8	Piece 8a	2 [3] strips, 6½″ wide
	Piece 8b	9 [16] rectangles, 2″ × 18″
Fabric 9	Piece 9	1 [2] strips, 11¼″ wide; crosscut into 5 [8] rectangles, 8¼″ × 11¼″

MAKE THE STRIP SETS

Use ¼″ seam allowances for all piecing.

1. For **pieces 2b–7a**, you will make a strip set and cut segments from it. Sew together 2 strip sets of **fabrics 2–7** in that order. Press all the seam allowances toward strip 2b.

2. Cut 9 [16] segments, each 5″ wide, across the strip sets. Set aside.

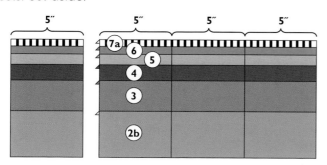

Cut segments from strip set.

CUT THE OTHER PIECES

The irregularly shaped pieces in the block—**1, 2a,** and **8a**—can be cut from strips using templates or the Tape-on-the-Ruler method. The instructions here are written using the Tape-on-the-Ruler method so you can try it. If you'd rather use templates, make the templates by referring to pages 17–18, cut the fabric, and skip to the section Cut Piece 9 on page 40.

Mark the straight of grain on each piece with arrows on the Master Cutting Guide. Keep the straight of grain along the outside edges of the blocks unless the pattern of your fabric dictates otherwise. If you are using a directional fabric, remember to draw grainline arrows on the templates or make note of the pattern direction when cutting strips for the Tape-on-the-Ruler method.

Cut Piece 1

1. Square up the left end of each of the 10˝ strips of **fabric 1** with a 90° cut.

2. Now you are ready to proceed with the Tape-on-the-Ruler cutting (see pages 18–21 as needed). Use the Master Cutting Guide to position your ruler and add tape reference lines before transferring the ruler to the fabric on your cutting mat to cut the piece.

Remember that reference lines are the lines representing the seams or cut edges that already exist on the fabric piece or strip set you are using. Reference lines for the first cut are usually based on the straight edges of fabric strips or a right-angle end of the strip, if one exists in the piece you are cutting. Such a right angle does exist in **piece 1.** The outside corner of the block will provide the reference lines. Position the corner of the cutting ruler on the Master Cutting Guide at the inside corner of **piece 1** so that the ruler extends ¼˝ beyond the drawn seamlines. Place strips of ½˝ tape right along the outside corner of the block and indicate "CUT EDGE" on the tape.

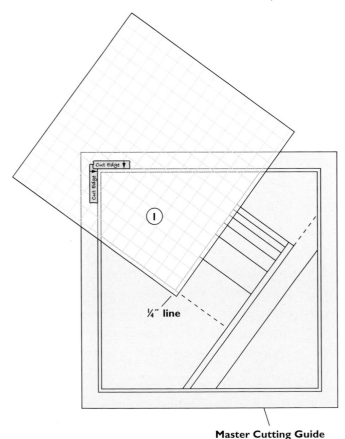

¼˝ line

Master Cutting Guide

Tape reference lines for piece 1.

3. Align the tape on the ruler with the 90° angle of the fabric 1 strip you have prepared. The remaining 2 edges form a right angle, and both can be cut around the corner of your ruler in one position. Cut one side, then the remaining side of **piece 1.**

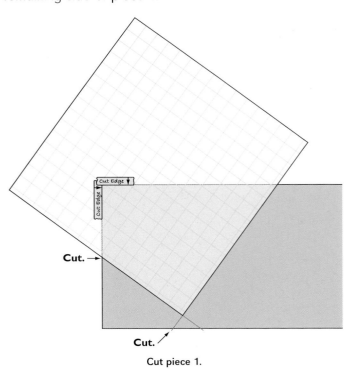

Cut. →

Cut.

Cut piece 1.

4. Compare your cut piece to its counterpart on the Master Cutting Guide to check accuracy.

5. To cut the remaining 8 [15] of **piece 1,** you can use the piece you just cut as a template and dovetail the cuts to make the most efficient use of your fabric. You can also cut another 90° angle across the end of the strip and use the taped ruler to cut the rest of the pieces, but this takes more fabric. When all the pieces are cut, stack them (right side up) on top of their place on the Master Cutting Guide. When you have oriented them in the correct position, transfer them to a holding area on your work-table. Label the stack if desired.

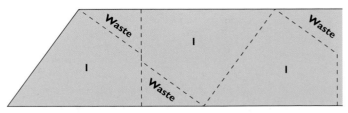

Dovetail the pieces for the most efficient use of the fabric.

Cut Piece 2a

1. Square up the left end of the 10″ **fabric 2** strips. This right angle will provide the first 2 sides of **piece 2a**.

2. Place the cutting edge of the ruler on the Master Cutting Guide along the next edge of **piece 2a** you want to cut. Since it has a right-angle corner within the block, you can use the corner of your 15″ square ruler at that point, positioning the edge of the ruler ¼″ beyond the lines of the inner corner. Then tape the outer corner as your reference point. Mark "CUT EDGE" on the tape.

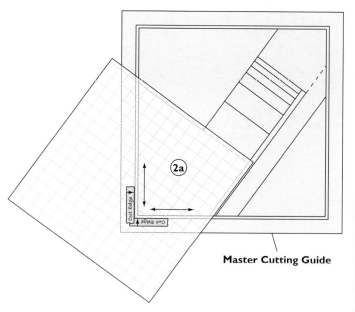

Tape references for piece 2a.

3. Move the taped ruler to the **fabric 2** strip on your cutting mat and align the tape with the right angle of the fabric strip. Cut the remaining sides of **piece 2a** along the edges of the ruler.

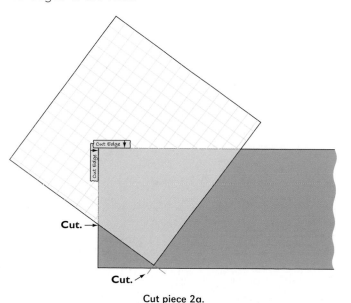

Cut. →

Cut. ↗

Cut piece 2a.

4. To cut the remaining 8 [15] of **piece 2**, use the piece you just cut as a template and dovetail the pieces across the fabric strip. You can also cut another 90° angle across the end of the strip and use the taped ruler to cut the rest of the pieces. Stack the cut pieces, right side up, and place them on top of the 2a position of the Master Cutting Guide in order to find the correct orientation. Transfer this stack to the holding area with the other pieces—in its proper relationship to them.

Cut Piece 8a

1. Position the ruler on the Master Cutting Guide, aligning the ¼″ lines with the drawn seamlines as shown. You'll want the grainline of the fabric to be parallel to the outside edges of the block for greatest stability.

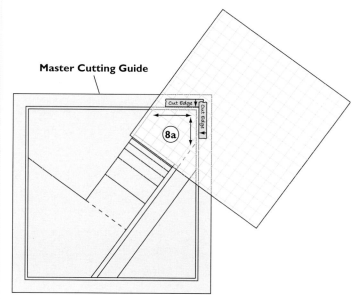

Tape reference points.

2. Square up 1 end of each 6½″ **fabric 8** strip. This will become the upper right square corner of the piece.

3. Align the taped reference point with the right angle of the fabric strip and cut 2 sides of **piece 8a** as you did for the other pieces.

4. Since this is a 5-sided piece you need to make 1 additional cut. (This is the side indicated by the dashed line.) Use your ruler to measure 5½″ from the slanted left edge of the piece and make a cut along the ruler as shown. Before you cut, confirm this measurement on your Master Cutting Guide by measuring across **piece 8a** and adding a ¼″ seam allowance on both sides (½″ total).

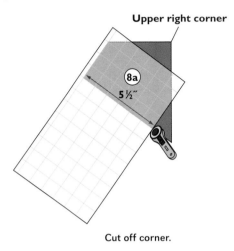

Cut off corner.

5. Continue to cut, dovetailing the pieces as you did before. Stack these cut pieces, right side up, and store them in your holding area in the correct position.

Cut Piece 9

Cut each of the 8¼″ × 11¼″ **fabric 9** rectangles in half diagonally from lower left corner to upper right corner as shown. Stack these triangles, right side up, in their proper place in the holding area. You need 9 [16] triangles for the blocks.

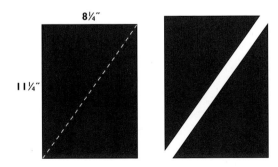

Cut rectangles into triangles.

CONSTRUCT THE BLOCKS

Use ¼″ seam allowances for all seams.

All the pieces for your blocks are cut and stacked in their proper relationship. Now it's time to construct the blocks. This block is easy. The pieces are simple shapes and the partial-seam technique makes construction simple. I like to use an assembly-line method, doing the same parts of all the blocks at the same time.

1. See Special Lesson: Partial Seams on the next page to sew **pieces 1** through **8a** together.

2. Sew **piece 8b** onto the unit made in Step 1 along the 7b–8a edge. Press the seam toward **8b**. Trim the ends of 8b so that its edges are even with the bottom edge of 2a and the right side of 8a as shown. This will help you position **piece 9**.

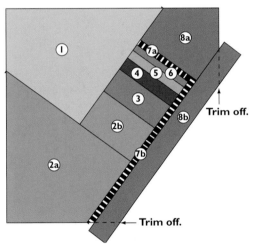

Trim the edges of piece 8b.

3. Add piece 9. Press the seam and the block is done! Don't worry if the outside edges are not exactly even. We'll trim them later.

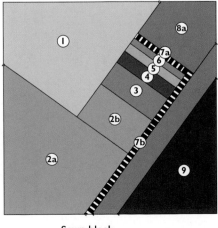

Sewn block

Partial Seams

Some pieced blocks, or parts of pieced blocks, go together more easily if you use the partial seam technique. Use this technique when you find that the sides of 2 adjoining pieces to be sewn together are not the same length until you add another piece.

For example, look at the block diagram on page 35 for this quilt. **Piece 7b** is sewn to the side of the **2b–7a** strip-pieced section, but the 2 are not the same length. **Piece 2b** is sewn to **piece 2a**, but their sides are not the same length either until **piece 1** is added. The strip-pieced section, **2b–7a**, is sewn to **piece 1** but the lengths of their sides are not the same, nor is the side of **piece 7a** the same length as **piece 8a** where these 2 connect. Sewing a partial seam is the perfect solution to avoid sewing set-in seams in each of these areas.

1. Sew strip **7b** to the strip-pieced section **2b–7a**, but **stop sewing when you get to about the middle of piece 2b.** The dot on the pattern on page 35 indicates the approximate stopping point. Press the seam toward the narrow strip.

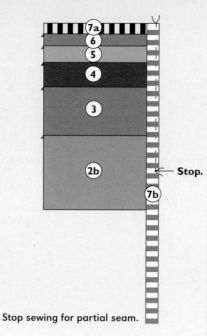

← Stop.

Stop sewing for partial seam.

2. Now the length of **piece 7a plus piece 7b** is the same length as **piece 8a.** Sew **piece 8a** to the pieced unit as shown. Press toward the piece just added.

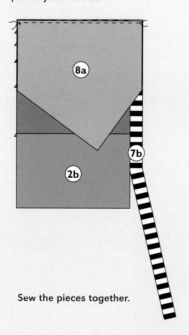

Sew the pieces together.

3. Work in a counterclockwise order and add the next 2 pieces, **piece 1** and **piece 2a**, pressing toward each newly added piece.

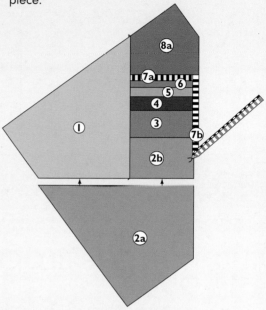

Sew the next two pieces.

4. Now you can sew **piece 7b** the rest of the way down to complete the seam as shown.

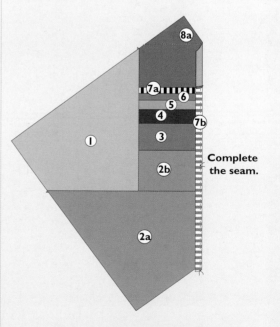

Complete the seam.

Now you can complete the seam.

SQUARE THE BLOCKS

Now that your blocks are pieced, it's important to trim them all to exactly 15″ square. The ½″ extra you added to all the outside edge pieces will ensure that you can get a full 15″ × 15″ block from your pieced blocks. (See Square Up the Blocks on page 24 to trim your blocks using a 15″ square ruler with tape as a reference.)

> ### Reminder
> *If the taped references on the 15″ square ruler don't match all the blocks exactly the same way, choose 1 or 2 references to match in all the blocks and trim the blocks around the edge of the 15″ ruler using 1 consistent reference point.*

AUDITION THE BLOCKS AS A QUILT

I always recommend looking at different ways to position or use the blocks before you decide to trim them to make a shifted image. Arrange the blocks in several different side-by-side settings first, photographing each as you try it.

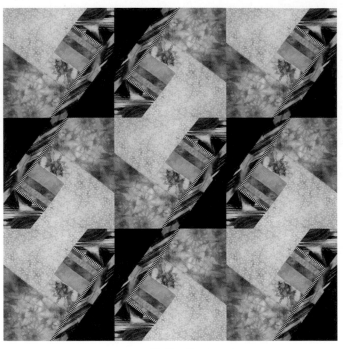

Option 2

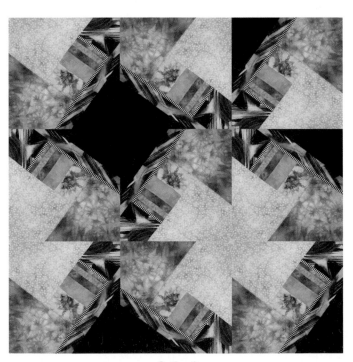

Option 3

Option 1

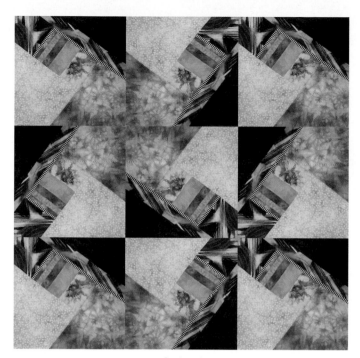

Option 4

Finally, check the blocks as a shifted image by using the diagram for the 9-block quilt on page 26 or the 16-block quilt on page 28. Fold under the parts to be trimmed and put them up on your design wall edge to edge, according to the diagram. Photograph this version as well.

Study the group of photos and decide which you like best. If you like the trimmed (folded under) version best, continue with Trim the Blocks for a Shifted Image below. If you prefer to use them as they are, go to Sew the Blocks Together.

TRIM THE BLOCKS FOR A SHIFTED IMAGE

For a shifted-image quilt, trim the blocks according to the diagram and trimming instructions on pages 26 or 28. I trimmed the nine blocks in my quilt to 12″ × 12″.

SEW THE BLOCKS TOGETHER

Sew each row of blocks together. Press the seam allowances in opposite directions from row to row. When you sew the rows together, the seams will butt up against each other and the seams will match nicely. I like to press the row seams open to distribute the bulk.

Stitch Carefully

Remember that there will be some bias edges on the outside edges of the blocks, so be careful to stitch them together without stretching the fabric. Pin often and use a walking foot to keep a bias edge from stretching and rippling, or use one of the other methods described on page 15.

MAKE THE BORDERS

See Borders on pages 31–33 to get ideas for bordering your quilt. Choose from one of the options there, design your own border, or complete your quilt with a border like mine, made from the trimmings that remained after cutting the 15″ blocks into 12″ blocks.

On the left side and top of the quilt, I added a strip of red-violet that finishes to ¼″ wide. The red-violet strips were pieced with short sections of scraps from the trimmings before being sewn to the quilt. The right side and the bottom of the quilt have uninterrupted strips of the cobalt blue that finish to ½″ wide. In the outer border I used trimmings that were cut from the blocks. The lightest trimmings were sewn around the upper left-hand side of the quilt to accentuate its "lightness," and the medium and dark trimmings were used in the darker bottom right-hand corner of the quilt.

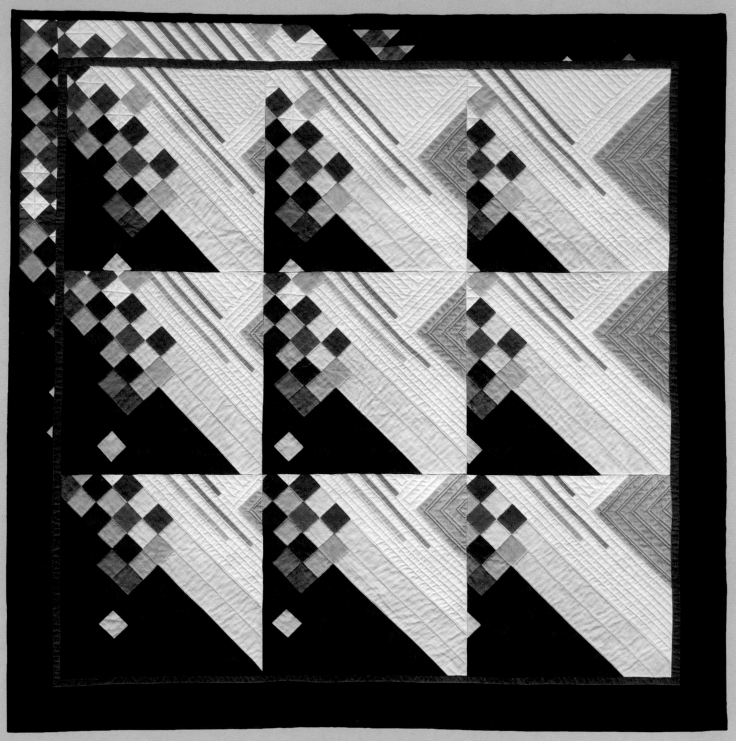

Cherrywood Checkerboard, 39³⁄₄″ × 39³⁄₄″, by Lorraine Torrence, quilted by Gretchen Engle, 2005

Easy Block

In this project, you will sew segments cut from strip sets in parallel diagonal rows all the way across the block. Keeping track of the color placement may be the most challenging part of making this block. Create a mock-up of the block to audition your fabrics and use it to keep track of your color choices.

This design is most effective when created with hand-dyed (or hand-dyed-like) fabrics that provide many gradations and subtle variations of each color. Solids or commercial mottled fabrics also work well. Again, notice that the opposite corners of the block are very different. Light is opposite dark and busy is opposite plain. I purposely did not try to balance the block with value placement because the balance is achieved with repetition; as the block is repeated across the quilt, the alternating dark and light areas do a fine job of balancing the quilt. (See Design Tip: Scale, Color, and Value, on page 47, for a discussion of other design features in this block.)

I have identified the fabrics in this quilt by number and color for easier reference. Substitute the color names with the colors you are using for each area of the block.

Cutting methods: For this quilt, you will use a combination of strip piecing and rotary cutting.

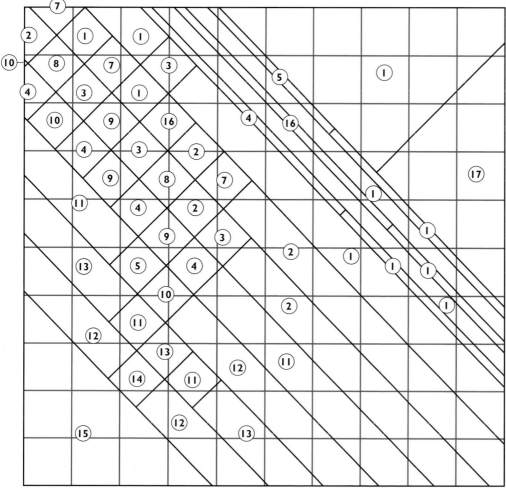

Block Diagram for Easy Block (10 × 10 grid)

Fabric Requirements

Yardage is based on 38"–40"-wide fabric to allow for hand-dyed fabrics that are often narrower.

Fabrics are listed by number and the color used in the quilt shown.

See page 5 for other supplies you will need.

Fabric	9-Block Quilt	16-Block Quilt
Fabric 1 (light green)	$1\frac{3}{8}$ yards	2 yards
Fabric 2 (light blue-green)	$\frac{3}{4}$ yard	$1\frac{1}{8}$ yards
Fabric 3 (bright green)	$\frac{1}{4}$ yard	$\frac{3}{8}$ yard
Fabric 4 (turquoise)	$\frac{1}{4}$ yard or fat quarter	$\frac{1}{2}$ yard
Fabric 5 (teal)	$\frac{1}{4}$ yard or fat quarter	$\frac{3}{8}$ yard
Fabric 6 (red)	$\frac{1}{8}$ yard	$\frac{1}{8}$ yard
Fabric 7 (red-orange)	$\frac{1}{4}$ yard	$\frac{1}{4}$ yard
Fabric 8 (light rust)	$\frac{1}{8}$ yard	$\frac{1}{4}$ yard
Fabric 9 (magenta)	$\frac{1}{4}$ yard	$\frac{1}{4}$ yard
Fabric 10 (light purple)	$\frac{1}{8}$ yard	$\frac{1}{4}$ yard
Fabric 11 (burgundy)	$\frac{1}{2}$ yard	$\frac{5}{8}$ yard
Fabric 12 (maroon)	$\frac{5}{8}$ yard	$\frac{3}{4}$ yard
Fabric 13 (purple)	$\frac{3}{8}$ yard	$\frac{1}{2}$ yard
Fabric 14 (chartreuse)	$\frac{1}{8}$ yard	$\frac{1}{8}$ yard
Fabric 15 (dark red-violet)	1 yard (includes extra for border)	$1\frac{1}{2}$ yards (includes extra for border)
Fabric 16 (medium blue)	$\frac{1}{4}$ yard or fat eighth	$\frac{3}{8}$ yard or fat quarter
Fabric 17 (orange)	$\frac{3}{8}$ yard	$\frac{5}{8}$ yard
Backing*	$2\frac{3}{4}$ yards	$3\frac{3}{8}$ yards
Batting*	49" × 49"	60" × 60"
Binding*	$\frac{1}{2}$ yard	$\frac{1}{2}$ yard

*Backing, batting, and binding quantities are approximate, based on: 15" blocks trimmed to 12" and sewn together without sashing; 4" borders added on all sides.

Design Tip: Scale, Color, and Value

*For more dynamic results, vary the size of pieces and areas when you are designing a block. Just as varied **scale** in printed fabric usually makes a quilt more interesting, so does varied **scale** in the size of the pieces in the block. In general, most good compositions have **big** spaces, **medium** spaces, and **small** spaces. The Easy block in this chapter is a good example of this. If your quilt blocks, and ultimately your quilts, are boring, ask yourself if it is because all the pieces are about the same size. If they are, try dividing up some spaces to add narrow or small pieces.*

*Another reason a quilt or block may look less interesting is because the **color palette** is limited or not broad enough in spectrum. Usually, rich **color** in a quilt is derived by using colors across the color wheel from each other—or, better yet, from all around the color wheel. This Easy block has a wide color range. Notice that all the greens are not the same green and all the purples are not the same purple. Some are cool; some are warm. Accent colors do not need to occupy a large area either. A little bit of a **color** with a lot of punch goes a long way to making the block exciting and dynamic.*

***Value**—the lightness or darkness of a color—is always an important consideration in every quilt or block design. If the **value** range in your work is not wide enough, meaning that the colors are too close in value, the quilt will look mushy and the design will be hard to read. Remember: **Value defines a composition.** Even if you are striving for a close-value quilt, there must be at least a little bit of contrast or your quilt will look like mush.*

Instructions

GETTING STARTED

1. Preshrink and iron your fabric.

2. Make a Master Cutting Guide following the instructions beginning on page 11. The block drawing on page 45 is divided into a grid of 10 divisions; transfer the design to a 15″ square divided into a 10 × 10 grid of 1½″.

3. Add a pencil line around the 15″ square Master Cutting Guide, ½″ outside the perimeter of the square.

4. Make a copy of your Master Cutting Guide and audition your fabric choices by cutting pieces and gluing them to the copy. Look at the mocked-up block through your Multi-View lens to see how it will repeat. This won't be an exact version of how it will look, but it will give you a good idea.

Follow the cutting instructions on the next page and the steps for making strip sets. I suggest you cut and sew fabrics for 1 diagonal row at a time. This will keep the strips organized, and you won't have to figure out which strip belongs in which strip set. Keep your mock-up handy to identify each row as you make it.

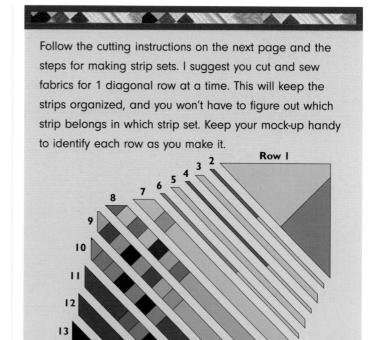

Construct the block in rows.

CUTTING

All cutting dimensions include ¼″ seam allowances.

Information specific to the 16-block quilt is given within brackets [ ].

Fabric	Number and Size to Cut	Second Cut
Row 1		
Fabric 1 (light green)	2 [4] squares, 12¼″ × 12¼″	Cut in half diagonally twice to make 8 [16] triangles*
Fabric 17 (orange)	2 [4] squares, 10¼″ × 10¼″	Cut in half diagonally twice to make 8 [16] triangles*
Row 2		
Fabric 1 (light green)	1 rectangle, 9″ × 7½″ [9″ × 13″]	—
Fabric 5 (teal)	1 rectangle, 8″ × 7½″ [8″ × 13″]	—
Row 3		
Fabric 1 (light green)	1 rectangle, 17″ × 10″ [1 square, 17″ × 17″]	9 [16] strips, 1″ × 17″
Row 4		
Fabric 16 (medium blue)	1 rectangle, 12″ × 7½″ [12″ × 13″]	—
Fabric 1 (light green)	1 rectangle, 6½″ × 7½″ [6½″ × 13″]	—
Row 5		
Fabric 1 (light green)	1 rectangle, 19″ × 10″ [19″ × 17″]	9 [16] strips, 1″ × 19″
Row 6		
Fabric 4 (turquoise)	1 rectangle, 10½″ × 7½″ [10½″ × 13″]	—
Fabric 1 (light green)	1 rectangle, 9½″ × 7½″ [9½″ × 13″]	—
Row 7		
Fabric 1 (light green)	1 rectangle, 4¼″ × 17″ [4¼″ × 30″]	—
	1 square, 17″ × 17″ [1 rectangle, 17″ × 30″]	—
Fabric 3 (bright green)	1 strip, 1¾″ × 17″ [1¾″ × 30″]	—
Row 8		
Fabric 7 (red-orange)	1 strip, 2¼″ × 17″ [2¼″ × 30″]	—
	2 strips, 1¾″ × 17″ [1¾″ × 30″]	—
Fabric 6 (red)	1 strip, 1¾″ × 17″ [1¾″ × 30″]	—
Fabric 1 (light green)	2 strips, 1¾″ × 17″ [1¾″ × 30″]	—
Fabric 2 (light blue-green)	1 strip, 1¾″ × 17″ [1¾″ × 30″]	—
	1 rectangle, 14″ × 17″ [14″ × 30″]	—
Row 9		
Fabric 2 (light blue-green)	1 strip, 2¼″ × 17″ [2¼″ × 30″]	—
	1 strip, 1¾″ × 17″ [1¾″ × 30″]	—
	1 rectangle, 12½″ × 17″ [12½″ × 30″]	—
Fabric 8 (light rust)	2 strips, 1¾″ × 17″ [1¾″ × 30″]	—

Fabric	Number and Size to Cut	Second Cut
Row 9 (Continued)		
Fabric 3 (bright green)	3 strips, $1\frac{3}{4}'' \times 17''$ [$1\frac{3}{4}'' \times 30''$]	—
Fabric 9 (magenta)	1 strip, $1\frac{3}{4}'' \times 17''$ [$1\frac{3}{4}'' \times 30''$]	—
Row 10		
Fabric 4 (turquoise)	4 strips, $1\frac{3}{4}'' \times 17''$ [$1\frac{3}{4}'' \times 30''$]	—
Fabric 10 (light purple)	2 strips, $1\frac{3}{4}'' \times 17''$ [$1\frac{3}{4}'' \times 30''$]	—
Fabric 9 (magenta)	2 strips, $1\frac{3}{4}'' \times 17''$ [$1\frac{3}{4}'' \times 30''$]	—
Fabric 11 (burgundy)	1 rectangle, $11\frac{1}{2}'' \times 17''$ [$11\frac{1}{2}'' \times 30''$]	—
Row 11		
Fabric 11 (burgundy)	1 rectangle, $6\frac{1}{2}'' \times 17''$ [$6\frac{1}{2}'' \times 30''$]	—
Fabric 5 (teal)	1 strip, $1\frac{3}{4}'' \times 17''$ [$1\frac{3}{4}'' \times 30''$]	—
Fabric 10 (light purple)	1 strip, $1\frac{3}{4}'' \times 17''$ [$1\frac{3}{4}'' \times 30''$]	—
Fabric 12 (maroon)	1 rectangle, $10'' \times 17''$ [$10'' \times 30''$]	—
Row 12		
Fabric 13 (purple)	2 rectangles, $6\frac{1}{2}'' \times 17''$ [$6\frac{1}{2}'' \times 30''$]	—
	1 strip, $1\frac{3}{4}'' \times 17''$ [$1\frac{3}{4}'' \times 30''$]	—
Fabric 11 (burgundy)	2 strips, $1\frac{3}{4}'' \times 17''$ [$1\frac{3}{4}'' \times 30''$]	—
Row 13		
Fabric 12 (maroon)	2 rectangles, $6'' \times 17''$ [$6'' \times 30''$]	—
Fabric 14 (chartreuse)	1 strip, $1\frac{3}{4}'' \times 17''$ [$1\frac{3}{4}'' \times 30''$]	—
Row 14		
Fabric 15 (dark red-violet)	4 [8] squares, $7\frac{3}{8}'' \times 7\frac{3}{8}''$	Cut diagonally once to make 8 [16] triangles*

*Note: For the 9-block quilt, use 1 of the triangles as a template to cut a 9th triangle. Make sure the hypotenuse (long side) of the triangle is on the straight of the grain for Row 1 and on the bias for Row 14.

MAKE THE STRIP SETS

Use ¼" seam allowances for all piecing.

1. Row 1 Sew the pairs of light green and orange triangles together on their short sides. The point of the light green triangle will extend below the orange one. Press the seams toward the orange.

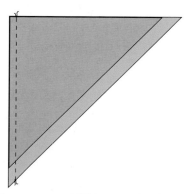

Sew orange and light green triangles together.

2. Row 2 Sew the light green rectangle to the teal rectangle on their 7½″ [13″] sides. Press the seams toward the teal. Make a pencil line on the back of the green fabric 1¼″ away from the seam. (See Special Lesson: Aligning Seams That Have No Reference Point, Part 2, on page 52.) Cut 9 [16] segments, each ¾″ wide, from the strip set.

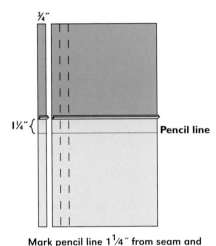

Mark pencil line 1¼″ from seam and cut segments.

3. Row 3 No piecing is required.

4. Row 4 Sew the light green rectangle to the medium blue rectangle on their 7½″ [13″] sides. Press the seam toward the medium blue. Draw a pencil line on the back of the teal 2″ from the seam. Cut 9 [16] segments, each ¾″ wide, from the strip set as you did for the previous 2-part strip.

5. Row 5 No piecing is required. Mark the reference points on the wrong side of the strip. Mark one point 10″ from the left edge along the top edge of the strip (it will be the bottom when you turn it over) and a second reference point 11½″ from the left edge along the bottom edge (it will be the top edge when you turn it over).

6. Row 6 Sew the light green rectangle to the turquoise rectangle on their 7½″ [13″] sides. Draw a line through the turquoise rectangle, 6¼″ to the left of the seam. Press the seam toward the turquoise. Cut 9 [16] segments, each ¾″ wide, from the strip set.

7. Row 7 Sew the 4¼″ light green rectangle to the bright green strip, then sew this unit to the 17″ light green rectangle on their 17″ [30″] sides. Press the seams toward the bright green. Cut 9 [16] segments, each 1¾″ wide, from the strip set.

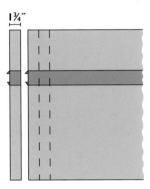

Cut segments from strip set.

8. Row 8 Sew a strip set in this order: 2¼″ red-orange strip, light green strip, 1¾″ red-orange strip, light green strip, red strip, 1¾″ light blue-green strip, 1¾″ red-orange strip, and 14″-wide blue-green strip, on their 17″ [30″] sides. Press the seams toward the reds and away from the greens. Cut 9 [16] segments, each 1¾″ wide, from the strip set.

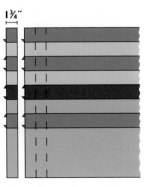

Cut segments from strip set.

9. Row 9 Sew a strip set in this order: light blue-green strip, rust strip, bright green strip, magenta strip, bright green strip, rust strip, light blue-green strip, bright green strip, and light blue-green rectangle, on their 17″ [30″] sides. Press the seam allowances toward the reds and away from the blue-green. Cut 9 [16] segments, each 1¾″ wide, from the strip set.

10. Row 10 Sew a strip set in this order: light purple strip, turquoise strip, light purple strip, turquoise strip, magenta strip, turquoise strip, magenta strip, turquoise strip, and burgundy rectangle, on their 17″ [30″] sides. Press the seam allowances toward the purples, magentas, and burgundy, and away from the turquoise. Cut 9 [16] segments, each 1¾″ wide, from the strip set.

11. Row 11 Sew a strip set in this order: burgundy rectangle, teal strip, light purple strip, and maroon rectangle, on their 17″ sides. Press the seams toward the burgundy and light purple, and away from the teal and maroon. Cut 9 [16] segments, each 1¾″ wide, from the strip set.

12. Row 12 Sew a strip set in this order: purple rectangle, burgundy strip, purple strip, burgundy strip, and purple rectangle, on their 17″ [30″] sides. Press the seams toward the purples. Cut 9 [16] segments, each 1¾″ wide, from the strip set.

13. Row 13 Sew a strip set in this order: maroon rectangle, chartreuse strip, and maroon rectangle. Press the seams toward the maroon. Cut 9 [16] segments, each 1¾″ wide, from the strip set.

14. Row 14 No piecing is required.

SEW THE ROWS TOGETHER

1. Arrange the cut rows in the order shown on the Master Cutting Guide.

2. Sew **Row 1** to **Row 2**. You will see that there is no seam reference point for aligning the seam in **Row 2** to the light green triangle in **Row 1**. The pencil line you drew on the back of the fabric when you made the strip set provides the reference point. Match the pencil line to the seam in Row 1 and sew the 2 rows together, assembly-line fashion, for all the blocks. Press the seam allowances toward the triangles.

3. Before sewing **Row 3** to **Row 2**, be sure to read Special Lesson: Sewing Very Even ¼″ Strips below. It is very important that the ¼″ finished strip be perfectly even. In a strip this narrow, any variation in width is very obvious and distracting. Center **Row 3** so that it extends evenly beyond **Row 2** at both ends, and sew **Row 2** to **Row 3**. Press the seam toward **Row 2**. Sew this combination in all the blocks.

4. Continue to add **Rows 4, 5, 6,** and **7** using the penciled reference points to line up your rows. Sew the narrow strips with the presser foot to the right of the seam as you did for **Rows 2** and **3**.

5. As you come to the rows with the checkerboard squares, refer to your fabric mock-up to remind you where to position the colors when sewing the rows together. Having pressed the seam allowances as the instructions for each strip set indicate, you should have opposing seams at each intersection on the checkerboard section. This makes matching these seams easy.

6. Add the final corner triangle row. Use the penciled reference point trick to find a point on the corner triangle to match to one of the seams of the chartreuse square for positioning purposes.

 SPECIAL LESSON:

Sewing Very Even ¼″ Strips

The easiest and most effective way to sew a strip that finishes to ¼″ wide (or any very narrow width) is to use the **left** edge of your presser foot for the second seam. Sewing the cut ³⁄₄″ strip to 1 strip is not difficult: keep the raw edges even and sew a ¼″ seam allowance.

1. Press the seam allowance away from the ³⁄₄″ strip so that it lies flat (see Rows 2 and 3 in the project block).

2. You can find a ¼″ seam allowance by using a ¼″ presser foot, both sides of which are exactly ¼″ from the needle when it is in the center position. Alternately, you may use the regular all-purpose foot and move your needle position to the right until it is ¼″ from

the right edge of the presser foot. Similarly, you can move the needle to the left until it is ¼″ from the left edge of the presser foot to sew with the presser foot on the left.

3. When you add the next strip, whatever its width, place the 2 strips with right sides together so that the raw edges are exactly even and the narrow strip is on top. Position the strips under your presser foot so that the **left** side of the presser foot is against the previously sewn seam. Since you pressed the seam allowance **away** from the narrow strip, this results in both thicknesses of the seam allowance being to the left of the presser foot and providing a little ridge against which your presser foot can ride.

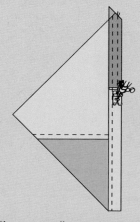

Place seam allowance against presser foot for narrow strip.

Keeping your presser foot against that ridge maintains a consistent width between the 2 lines of stitching on the narrow strip, resulting in a very even finished strip. You can change your needle position with an all-purpose foot to get different widths of narrow strips. Press the second seam allowance toward the narrow strip.

Aligning Seams That Have No Reference Point, Part 2

Some blocks, such as the Easy block in this quilt, contain seams that need to be positioned as designed even when there isn't another seam with which to align them.

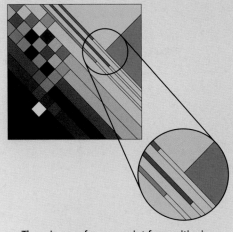

There is no reference point for positioning any of these seams.

The seam that connects the orange triangle and the light green triangle in the upper right of the block needs to

connect to the adjacent narrow strip at a specific place—the same place in every block—but there is no visual reference point. There is a way to make this matching job easy and consistently accurate.

In this block, you need to make a pencil mark on the back of the narrow green strip to match to the orange-to-green seamline in the first section. On the Master Cutting Guide, measure the distance between the orange-to-green seam in Row 1 and the teal-to-green seam in the next row. On the back of the narrow teal/light green fabric strip that is Row 2, measure that same distance from the seamline toward the light green and make a mark. Match this mark to the orange-to-green seamline.

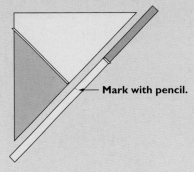

← Mark with pencil.

Mark on wrong side to match orange-to-green seam.

Since there will be several of the same matches to be made in the quilt, and all the light green strips are cut from a rectangle, an even easier solution would be to draw a line, parallel to the seamline, in the light green rectangle the proper measurement from the seam that connects the teal rectangle **before** the narrow strips are cut from the strip set. Then the line will be there ready to match to the orange-to-green seam in the first row every time you sew it!

Pencil line

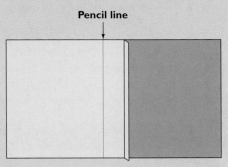

Draw line on strip set before cutting segments.

SQUARE THE BLOCKS

Review Square Up the Blocks on page 24. You may find that your Master Cutting Guide seamlines and the seamlines of your sewn blocks do not match as well as you thought they would. This is probably because there are 13 parallel seams in this block. Every seam is a chance for discrepancy, and even the most careful sewer will have a hard time maintaining a perfect block size. Instead of taping reference points using the Master Cutting Guide, use 1 of the angles in a fabric block as a reference. Choose a prominent angle in the block where

you can add 2 pieces of tape to the ruler to create a reference point so each block will be trimmed the same. Square up the blocks to 15″ × 15″.

AUDITION THE BLOCKS AS A QUILT

I always recommend looking at different ways to position or use the blocks before you decide to trim them to make a shifted image. Arrange the blocks in several different side-by-side settings first, photographing each as you try it.

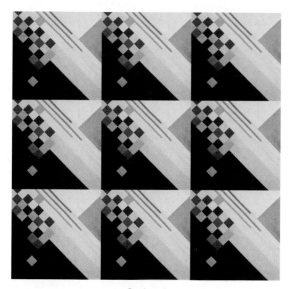

Option 1

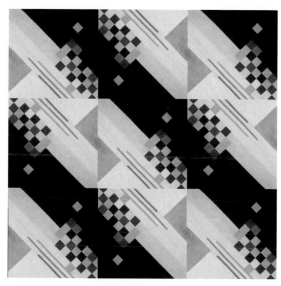

Option 2

Option 3

Finally, check the blocks as a shifted image by using the diagram for the 9-block quilt on page 26 or the 16-block quilt on page 28. Fold under the parts to be trimmed and put them up on your design wall, edge to edge, according to the diagram. Photograph this version as well.

Study the group of photos and decide which you like best. If you like the trimmed (folded under) version best, continue with Trim the Blocks for a Shifted Image below. If you prefer to use them as they are, skip the next section and sew the blocks together.

TRIM THE BLOCKS FOR A SHIFTED IMAGE

See The Shifted Image starting on page 25 and trim the blocks according to the diagram and trimming instructions for either the 9-block quilt or the 16-block quilt. I trimmed my blocks to 12″.

SEW THE BLOCKS TOGETHER

Sew each row of blocks together. Press the seam allowances in opposite directions from row to row. When you sew the rows together, the seams will butt up against each other and the seams will match nicely. I like to press the row seams open to distribute the bulk.

I made the 9-block quilt as shown on page 44, but I liked one of the other arrangements so much that I made another set of 16 blocks in different fabrics and arranged them as whole blocks without trimming them. That quilt is shown on page 82. Since there were no block trimmings to make a border on the 16-block quilt, I had to design and make a border for the second quilt the "old-fashioned" way.

MAKE THE BORDERS

Put your quilt up on your design wall and use your block trimmings to design a border (see Borders on pages 31–33). Remember that it is not necessary to use all of the trimmings, to use them in their original size, or to use them at all. Place them around your quilt in various arrangements and combinations until you find a successful result. Or look at the quilt photo on page 44 to complete your quilt with a similar border.

Industrial Shift, 50˝ × 50˝, by Lorraine Torrence, 2005

Intermediate Block

The Intermediate block is really fairly easy, just a bit more time consuming. To increase the challenge, I've made the sample a 16-block quilt instead of a 9-block quilt, but yardage and block-trimming information are included for a 9-block version. Once again, notice that the opposite corners contrast with each other in value (darkness and lightness), color (dull neutrals and bright color), and scale (small, busy piecing and large, empty open space).

Cutting methods: For this quilt, you will use a combination of templates and strip piecing.

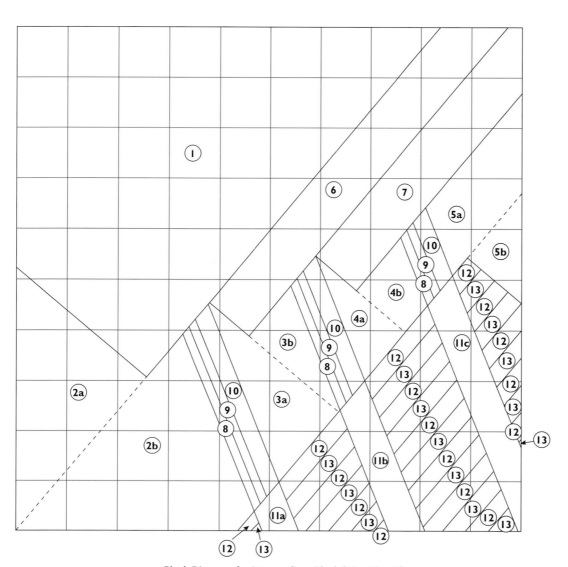

Block Diagram for Intermediate Block (10 × 10 grid)

Fabric Requirements

Yardage is based on 42"-wide fabric.

Fabrics are listed by number and the value and visual texture used in the quilt shown. See page 5 for other supplies you will need.

Note: *This design works well if fabrics 2, 3, 4, and 5 are light to dark values of the same fabric in the same color, that is, gradations of one color of fabric. I used very light gray to nearly black.*

Fabric	16-Block Quilt	9-Block Quilt
Fabric 1 (medium dark geometric)	2 yards	$1\frac{3}{8}$ yards
Additional for border (optional)	$\frac{1}{2}$ yard	$\frac{1}{4}$ yard
Fabric 2 (very light, mottled texture)	$1\frac{1}{4}$ yards	$\frac{3}{4}$ yard
Fabric 3 (medium light, mottled texture)	$\frac{3}{8}$ yard	$\frac{1}{4}$ yard
Fabric 4 (medium, mottled texture)	$\frac{1}{2}$ yard	$\frac{3}{8}$ yard
Fabric 5 (dark, mottled texture)	$\frac{5}{8}$ yard	$\frac{3}{8}$ yard
Fabric 6 (medium dark, colorful geometric)	$\frac{3}{8}$ yard	$\frac{1}{4}$ yard
Fabric 7 (medium light, colorful geometric)	$\frac{3}{8}$ yard	$\frac{1}{4}$ yard
Fabric 8 (bright color, small-scale print)	$\frac{1}{4}$ yard	$\frac{1}{4}$ yard
Fabric 9 (bright color, small-scale print) (Yardage includes enough extra for border.)	$\frac{1}{4}$ yard	$\frac{1}{4}$ yard
Fabric 10 (bright color, small-scale print)	$\frac{3}{8}$ yard	$\frac{1}{4}$ yard
Fabric 11 (dark print)	$\frac{1}{2}$ yard	$\frac{3}{8}$ yard
Additional for border and binding	$\frac{3}{4}$ yard	$\frac{2}{3}$ yard
Fabric 12 (colorful large-scale print)	1 yard	$\frac{5}{8}$ yard
Fabric 13 (colorful large-scale print, different colors from fabric 12)	1 yard	$\frac{5}{8}$ yard
Backing*	3 yards	$1\frac{1}{4}$ yards
Batting*	54" × 54"	44" × 44"
Binding*	$\frac{1}{2}$ yard	$\frac{1}{2}$ yard

*Backing, batting, and binding quantities are approximate, based on: 15" blocks trimmed to $10\frac{1}{2}$" and sewn together without sashing; 4" borders added on all sides.

Instructions

GETTING STARTED

1. Preshrink and iron your fabric.

2. Make a Master Cutting Guide following the instructions beginning on page 11. The block drawing on page 55 is divided into a grid of 10 divisions; transfer the design to a 15" square divided into a 10 x 10 grid of 1½".

3. Remember to add a pencil line around the 15" square cutting guide, ½" outside the perimeter of the square.

NOTE: Check your enlarged drawing and make corrections if it deviates from the following measurements.

- Pieces 6 and 7 are intended to finish to 1½" wide.

- Pieces 8 and 9 are intended to finish to ¼" wide.

- Piece 10 is intended to finish to ½" wide.

- Pieces 11a, b, and c are intended to finish to 1" wide.

- Pieces 12 and 13 are intended to finish to ½" wide.

4. Make a copy of your Master Cutting Guide and audition your fabric choices by cutting pieces and gluing them to the copy. Look at the mocked-up block through your Multi-View lens to see how it will repeat. This won't be an exact version of how it will look, but it can give you a good idea.

CUTTING

All cutting dimensions include ¼" seam allowances.

Cutting information specific to a 9-block quilt is given within brackets [ ].

Fabric	Used for	Number and Size to Cut
Fabric 8	Strip set 8–9–10	9 [5] strips, ¾" × 42"
Fabric 9	Strip set 8–9–10	9 [5] strips, ¾" × 42"
Fabric 10	Strip set 8–9–10	9 [5] strips, 1" × 42"
Fabric 3	Piece 3b	3 [2] strips, 2½" × 42"
Fabric 4	Piece 4a	3 [2] strips, 2½" × 42"
	Piece 4b	2 [1] strips, 2½" × 42"
Fabric 5	Piece 5a	2 [1] strips, 5¼" × 42"
Fabric 12	Strip set 12–13	28 [21] strips, 1" × 42"*
Fabric 13	Strip set 12–13	24 [18] strips, 1" × 42"*

* Keep the strips in order so you can still see the design of the fabric.

MAKE THE STRIP SETS

1. Sew 1 each of **strips 8, 9, and 10** together to make a strip set. Press the seams toward **fabric 10**. Repeat until you have made 9 [5] strip sets of this **8-9-10** combination. Set these aside.

(See Special Lesson: Sewing Very Even ¼″ Strips on page 51 and Special Lesson: Sewing Straight Strip Sets on page 60.)

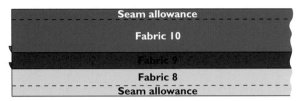

Strip set of fabrics 8-9-10

2. Sew a **fabric 3** strip to the **fabric 8** side of an **8-9-10** strip set you just made. Then sew a **fabric 4** strip to the **fabric 10** side of the strip set. Press the seams to one side. Repeat to make 2 [1] more strip sets like this. Set aside.

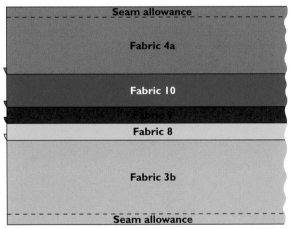

Strip set 3b-8-9-10-4a

3. Sew a **fabric 4** strip to the **fabric 8** edge of an **8-9-10** strip set, offsetting it as shown. Then add a **fabric 5** strip to the other side as shown. Press the seams to one side. Make a total of 2 [1] strip sets. Set aside.

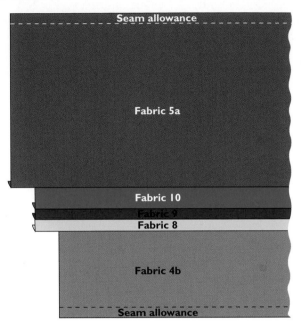

Strip set 4b-8-9-10-5a

4. Sew a strip set of the first 7 **fabric 12** strips alternated with the first 6 **fabric 13** strips. Begin and end with a **fabric 12** strip. Sew these strips together in order (see Special Lesson: Sewing Straight Strip Sets on page 60). Press the seams open. Make 3 [2] more of these strip sets, keeping the strips in order. Set aside.

NOTE: Because the strips finish to ½″ and the amount of seam allowance lost from sewing each strip is ½″, the pattern of each fabric appears to keep its original design between the interruptions of the alternate fabric. If you focus on fabric 12, you will still see its design. If you focus on fabric 13, you will still see its design.

MAKE THE TEMPLATES

1. To make freezer-paper templates, trace your block drawing from the Master Cutting Guide onto freezer paper, including the seamlines. You can also make cardboard or plastic templates using the method described on page 17. No matter which template material you choose, keep the following pieces together as one template. These will be used to cut pieces from the strip sets.

- Pieces 8-9-10 from the 2b-8-9-10-3a section

- Pieces 3b-8-9-10-4a

- Pieces 4b-8-9-10-5a

- All 4 of the piece 12-13-12-13 sections

2. If you are using freezer-paper templates, make notations at each edge of each template indicating the amount of extra fabric to add when cutting—¼" for seam allowances on inside edges or ½" on outside edges. Make sure each area on the freezer paper is marked with the number of the fabric to be cut.

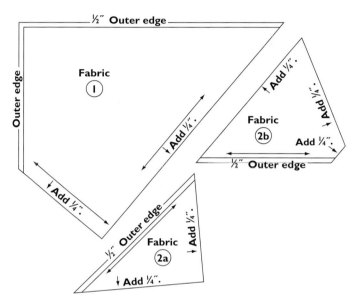

Mark each template with all the information you will need.

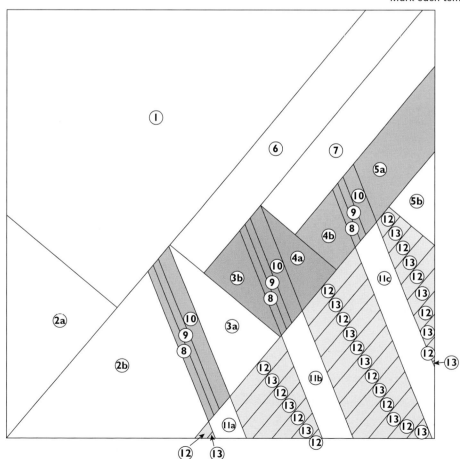

Cut each of the shaded sections as one template.

Sewing Straight Strip Sets

Sewing many strips together can often result in a curved strip set, sometimes even a ruffled strip set. There are several approaches to preventing this, including sewing with a walking foot and sewing one seam in one direction and the next seam in the opposite direction until you have sewn them all together in alternating directions. I use the following method. It is especially useful when I want to retain the pattern or print in a fabric that is sewn between strips of an alternate fabric.

1. Press the first 2 strips and place them, right sides together and raw edges aligned, on your ironing board. Smooth them out so they are neither stretched nor scrunched.

2. Pin them together with at least 9 pins spaced evenly. Stitch them together using a $\frac{1}{4}''$ seam allowance. Press the seam open.

3. Place the third strip next to the first 2, with right sides up so you can see that the pattern in strips 1 and 3 are aligned. Then flip strip 3 over on top of the second strip, right sides together and raw edges aligned, without moving the strip from its aligned position. Pin both ends together. Pick the strips up to see if the first and second sewn-together strips sag below the third strip or have stretched longer than the third strip.

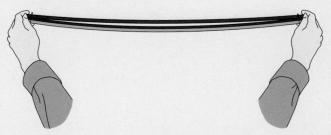

Compare length of first two strips to third.

4. If they are not the same length (sometimes the sewing and the pressing of the seam will stretch the strips), stretch the combination from both ends until the layers are even. Lower the combination onto the ironing board, keeping the strips stretched. Hold the left end of the strips in your left hand on the ironing board, and walk the fingers of your right hand up to the center of the strip and hold it together there until you can put a pin in the middle. Continue this stretching and pinning until you have about 9 pins in the strips.

Pin third strip in strip set, keeping it properly aligned.

5. Sew the seam with a $\frac{1}{4}''$ seam allowance and press the seam open.

6. Continue to add strips, aligning the pattern of each strip with the last strip of the same fabric. Pin the ends and several places in between by lifting the strips off the ironing board and stretching them until they are even and then pinning where the strips are aligned.

CUT THE BLOCK PIECES

Now that you have all your fabric prepared, strip sets sewn, and templates made, you are ready to cut out the pieces of the blocks.

1. Start with **piece 1**, referring to your Master Cutting Guide. If your fabric has a directional pattern, decide how you want it to be oriented in the block. I chose to make the straight of grain square with the inside right angle of the block, not the outside edges. Of course, if there is no visual reason to do this, it is better to have the straight of grain on the outside edges of the block. Having bias edges on your blocks means that you have to handle them carefully and not stretch the edges or distort the blocks. Mark the pattern piece with grainline arrows.

2. Because **piece 1** is asymmetrical, remember that you cannot fold your fabric to cut these pieces out. That would result in mirror-image pieces that would not be usable, unless your fabric is the same on both sides!

Cut out 16 [9] of **piece 1**. (See Cutting with Templates on pages 17–18 as needed.) Remember to pay attention to the notations for both grainline and seam allowance additions written on your templates. Below is a suggested cutting layout.

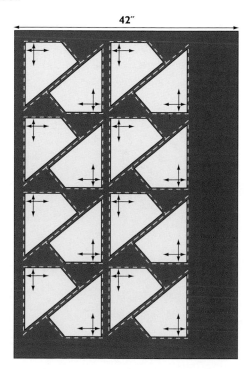

Suggested cutting layout for **piece 1**

3. Cut out all the single (not combination) pieces for the block using your templates. If the fabric does not have a directional pattern, position the templates so the grainline is parallel to the edges of the block.

4. Now it's time to cut the combination pieces. Begin with the **3b-8-9-10-4a** strip set. Place the template for this combination on the strip set so that the lines on the template are aligned with the seams. Iron the freezer-paper template in place or draw around the plastic or cardboard one.

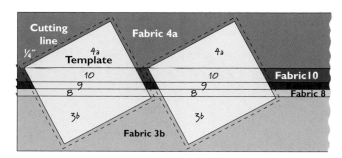

Placement of template on strip set

Cut ¼" beyond the freezer-paper template or on the line you drew around the plastic or cardboard template. Cut all 16 [9] of the pieces using this template. Then cut out the other combination pieces **except those to be cut from the 12–13 strip sets.**

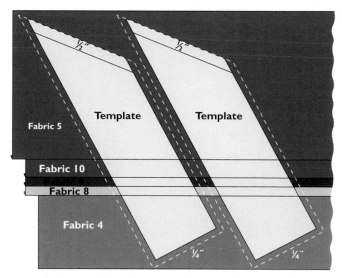

Placement of template on strip set

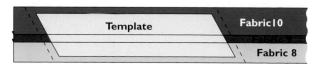

Placement of template on strip set

5. For the **piece 12-13 strip set**, iron the freezer-paper templates for all 4 of the pieces onto the strip set. Position the patterns on the strip set so they are **1"** apart. You will be inserting a 1" strip between each of these strip-pieced pieces, so you will not see that part of the pattern, and your patterned fabric will appear to be continuing behind the interruptions of the 1" pieces. If you are using plastic or cardboard templates, separate the templates by ½" because the ¼" seam allowance is already included in the template.

Placement of freezer-paper templates on strip set

Note: You will be wasting ½" of fabric between each of the templates. You may place the templates closer together and not waste the ½", but your patterned fabric will appear to be separated and the fabric print will not continue across the block. If this doesn't bother you, don't waste the fabric!

6. Cut out the pieces. For freezer paper cut ¼" beyond the inside edges of the templates. Cut even with the template on the outside edges as the extra ½" is already added. Keep the pieces together for 1 block. Repeat, but rotate the strip set and press the templates on the other edge to make the most efficient use of your fabric. You should be able to cut pieces for 4 blocks from each strip set.

CONSTRUCT THE BLOCKS

All seams are sewn with ¼" seam allowances.

With all your pattern pieces cut, you are ready to assembly-line piece the parts together.

1. Sew **piece 1** to **piece 2a**. Repeat to sew this seam for all 16 [9] blocks. Press the seam toward **piece 1** and set these units aside.

2. Sew **piece 7** to **piece 4b-8-9-10-5a**. Repeat for all the blocks. Press the seams toward **piece 7**.

Add piece 7 to 4b-8-9-10-5a.

3. Add **piece 3b-8-9-10-4a** to the unit from Step 2. Repeat for all the blocks and press the seams open.

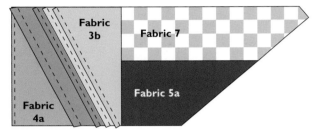

Add piece 3b-8-9-10-4a.

4. Sew **piece 6** to the unit from Step 3. Press the seams toward **piece 6**. Set these units aside.

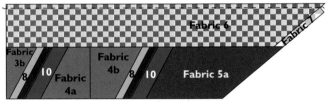

Add piece 6.

5. Sew **piece 2b** to **piece 8-9-10**, using the left-side-of-the-presser-foot trick to keep piece **8** even (see Special Lesson: Sewing Very Even ¼" Strips on page 51). Add **piece 3a**. Press the seams. Set the units aside.

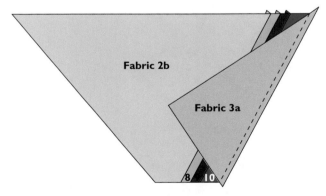

Add pieces 2b and 3a to 8-9-10.

6. Now you will sew the lower right corner section of the block. Lay out sets of **piece 12–13** with **pieces 11a, 11b,** and **11c** between them, referring to your Master Cutting Guide. Sew the series together. Add **piece 5b** to the squared end of the unit. Repeat to sew the other blocks.

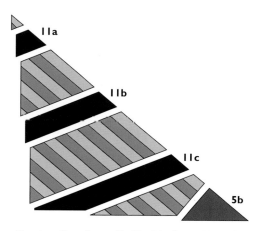

Sew together pieces 12–13 with pieces 11a, 11b, 11c, and 5b.

7. You now have completed the 3 diagonal rows that will go together to make the block. Before you sew the long seams, notice that in sewing the first 2 rows together, there is no reference point on **piece 1** for matching the **3a-to-6-3b** seam in the middle row. Make a mark in the seam allowance 3″ from the **1–2a** seamline on the wrong side of piece 1. (See Special Lesson: Aligning Seams That Have No Reference Point Part 2, page 52, for further details if needed.) Align the mark with the **3a–6** seamline. Sew the seam and press toward **piece 1.**

8. Adding the last row, the corner, will require a bit of precision to make the seams of the 1″-wide **piece 11s** match those of the 1″-wide **pieces 8-9-10.** Place the corner row on top of the middle row, right sides together. At the ¼″ seamline put a pin through the seamline of the first **piece 11** seam. Make the pin come out on the bottom layer at the seamline of **pieces 8-9-10** where it crosses the ¼″ seamline of the row.

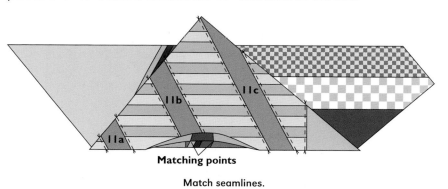

Matching points

Match seamlines.

9. Pin all the intersections of this seam. Stitch across the 3 intersections with a machine basting stitch. Open up the seam and see if the seams match to your satisfaction. If they do, sew the whole seam with a regular-length stitch. If they don't, it will be easy to take out a few basting stitches and reposition the layers before stitching again.

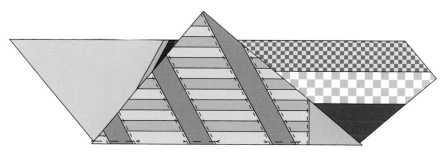

Machine baste matching points in the seam.

10. Match the intersections in all these seams and stitch them. Press the seams toward the corner.

Pressing Seams

The direction you press seams can be purposeful or arbitrary.

■ If one fabric is very dark and its neighbor is light, it is logical to press the seam toward the dark fabric so you won't see the dark fabric through the lighter one.

■ If there are several seams coming into the seam on one side and no seams in the neighboring fabric, it is logical to press the seam toward the fabric with no seams so the seam allowances in the pieced fabric won't have to double back on themselves.

■ If you are trying to match seams at an intersection, it is often easier to press the 2 intersecting seams in opposite directions so you create opposing—or interlocking—seams at the intersection.

■ If several of these scenarios coincide, you may just have to pick the solution that works best.

■ If none of these scenarios applies, then it's an arbitrary choice. If I suggest that you press a seam a certain way and it seems better to you to do it differently—go for it! Remember: There is more than one right way to do everything!

SQUARE THE BLOCKS

Now that your blocks are pieced, it's important to trim them all to exactly 15″ square. The ½″ extra you added to all the outside edge pieces will ensure that you can get a full cut 15″ block from your pieced blocks. (See the instructions on page 24 to square up your blocks using tape on the 15″ square ruler as a reference.)

If the taped references on the 15″ square ruler don't match all the blocks exactly the same way, choose 1 or 2 references to match in all blocks and trim the blocks around the edge of the 15″ ruler using 1 consistent reference point.

AUDITION THE BLOCKS AS A QUILT

I always recommend looking at different ways to position or use the blocks before you decide to trim them to make a shifted image. Try the blocks in several different side-by-side settings, photographing each as you try it.

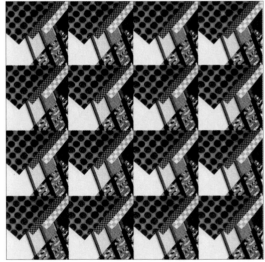

Option 1

Option 2

Option 3

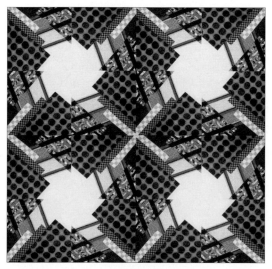

Option 4

Finally, check the blocks as a shifted image by using the diagram for the 9-block quilt on page 26 or the 16-block quilt on pages 27 or 28. Fold under the parts to be trimmed and put them up on your design wall, edge to edge, according to the diagram. Photograph this version as well.

Study the group of photos and decide which you like best. If you like the trimmed (folded under) version best, continue with Trim the Blocks for a Shifted Image below. If you prefer to use them as they are, skip the next section and sew the blocks together.

TRIM THE BLOCKS FOR A SHIFTED IMAGE

For a shifted-image quilt, label and trim the blocks according to the diagram and trimming instructions on pages 26–28. I trimmed my blocks to 10½".

SEW THE BLOCKS TOGETHER

Sew each row of blocks together. Press the seam allowances in opposite directions from row to row. When you sew the rows together, the seams will butt up against each other and the seams will match nicely. I like to press the row seams open to distribute the bulk.

MAKE THE BORDERS

When I auditioned the trimmings for a border on my design wall, they made the quilt look quite busy. I decided to use just a few of them and fill in the rest of the border with a fairly large proportion of fabric 1 as well as some plain fabric 2. I also decided to add 2 inner borders to separate the body of the quilt from the pieced border. I used 1½" strips of fabric 11 and ¾" strips of fabric 9 so that they finish to 1" and ¼". A simple fabric 11 binding is a good choice for this quilt too. One last decision: I used option 1 but I liked the whole thing better turned upside down!

Checkerboard Transitions, 49³/₄″ × 50″, by Lorraine Torrence, quilted by Gretchen Engle, 2005

Advanced Block

This project is not so much more difficult as it is more time consuming. More piecing, more blocks, and a checkerboard feature make this an interesting project for the more experienced quilter. Also notice the illusion of transparency in the upper right corner of the block. This is technically simple but requires careful selection of fabric to carry off the illusion.

A special design feature of this quilt is that the block changes almost entirely as it shifts from the upper left corner of the quilt to the lower right corner. The more blocks you have in your quilts and the more you cut off the blocks as you trim them, the more likely it is that this will happen. Of course, you must also begin with a block that is drastically different in opposite corners. For this 25-block quilt, the original 15″ blocks were trimmed to 9″.

Cutting methods: Use a combination of templates, templates placed on cut strips, and strip piecing.

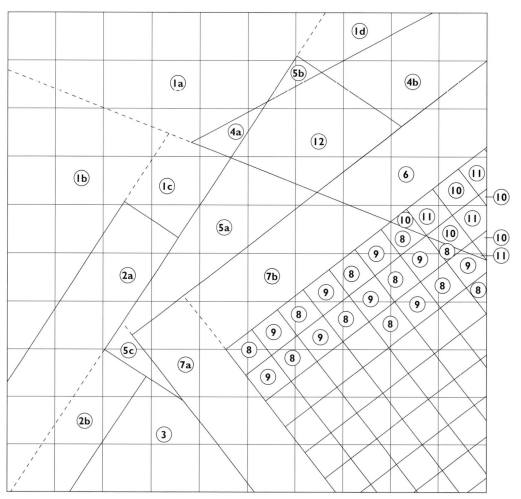

Block Diagram for Advanced Block (10 × 10 grid)

Fabric Requirements

Yardage is based on 42″-wide fabric.

Fabrics are listed by number, value, and the color used in the quilt shown.

See page 5 for other supplies you will need.

Fabric	25-Block Quilt	9-Block Quilt	16-Block Quilt
Fabric 1 (very light) Off-white	2$\frac{1}{4}$ yards	1$\frac{1}{8}$ yards	1$\frac{3}{4}$ yards
Fabric 2 (medium) Medium green	1 yard	$\frac{1}{2}$ yard	$\frac{3}{4}$ yard
Fabric 3 (dark) Purple	$\frac{2}{3}$ yard	$\frac{3}{8}$ yard	$\frac{1}{2}$ yard
Fabric 4 (light) Gold	$\frac{3}{4}$ yard	$\frac{1}{3}$ yard	$\frac{1}{2}$ yard
Fabric 5 (medium dark) Blue print	$\frac{3}{4}$ yard	$\frac{1}{3}$ yard	$\frac{1}{2}$ yard
Fabric 6 (medium light mix of 4 and 7) Medium light green	$\frac{1}{2}$ yard	$\frac{1}{4}$ yard	$\frac{3}{8}$ yard
Fabric 7 (medium) Blue	1 yard	$\frac{1}{2}$ yard	$\frac{3}{4}$ yard
Fabric 8 (medium bright) Bright blue	1$\frac{7}{8}$ yards	$\frac{7}{8}$ yard	1$\frac{1}{4}$ yards
Fabric 9 (medium bright to contrast with fabric 8) Bright red	1$\frac{7}{8}$ yards	$\frac{7}{8}$ yard	1$\frac{1}{4}$ yards
Fabric 10 (bright mix of 8 and 4) Bright green	$\frac{1}{2}$ yard	$\frac{1}{4}$ yard	$\frac{3}{8}$ yard
Fabric 11 (bright mix of 9 and 4) Bright orange	$\frac{1}{2}$ yard	$\frac{1}{4}$ yard	$\frac{3}{8}$ yard
Fabric 12 (bright mix of 5 and 4) Green print	$\frac{5}{8}$ yard	$\frac{1}{4}$ yard	$\frac{3}{8}$ yard
Backing*	3$\frac{1}{4}$ yards	1$\frac{1}{8}$ yards	2$\frac{3}{4}$ yards
Batting*	57″ × 57″	40″ × 40″	48″ × 48″
Binding*	$\frac{1}{2}$ yard	$\frac{3}{8}$ yard	$\frac{1}{2}$ yard

*Backing, batting, and binding quantities are approximate, based on: 15″ blocks trimmed to 9″ and sewn together without sashing; 4″ borders added on all sides.

Instructions

GETTING STARTED

1. Preshrink and iron your fabric

2. Make a Master Cutting Guide following the instructions beginning on page 67. The block drawing on page 11 is divided into a grid of 10 divisions; transfer the design to a 15″ square divided into a 10 x 10 grid of 1½″.

3. Add a pencil line around the 15″ square Master Cutting Guide, ½″ outside the perimeter of the square.

4. Make a copy of your Master Cutting Guide and audition your fabric choices by cutting pieces and gluing them to the copy. Look at the mocked-up block through your Multi-View lens to see how it will repeat. This won't be an exact version of how it will look, but it can give you a good idea.

CUTTING

Cut all strips across the width of the fabric (42").

Fabric	Used for	25-Block Quilt	9-Block Quilt	16-Block Quilt
Fabric 8	Checkerboard strip set	41 strips, $1\frac{1}{2}$" wide	18 strips, $1\frac{1}{2}$" wide	27 strips, $1\frac{1}{2}$" wide
Fabric 9	Checkerboard strip set	40 strips, $1\frac{1}{2}$" wide	18 strips, $1\frac{1}{2}$" wide	27 strips, $1\frac{1}{2}$" wide
Fabric 10	Checkerboard strip set	9 strips, $1\frac{1}{2}$" wide	3 strips, $1\frac{1}{2}$" wide	6 strips, $1\frac{1}{2}$" wide
Fabric 11	Checkerboard strip set	10 strips, $1\frac{1}{2}$" wide	4 strips, $1\frac{1}{2}$" wide	7 strips, $1\frac{1}{2}$" wide
Fabric 1	Piece 1c	3 strips, $2\frac{1}{2}$" wide	1 strip, $2\frac{1}{2}$" wide	2 strips, $2\frac{1}{2}$" wide
Fabric 2	Piece 2a	7 strips, $2\frac{1}{2}$" wide	3 strips, $2\frac{1}{2}$" wide	4 strips, $2\frac{1}{2}$" wide
	Piece 2b	5 strips, 2" wide	2 strips, 2" wide	3 strips, 2" wide
Fabric 6	Piece 6	5 strips, $2\frac{1}{2}$" wide	2 strips, $2\frac{1}{2}$" wide	4 strips, $2\frac{1}{2}$" wide
Fabric 7	Piece 7a	7 strips, $2\frac{1}{2}$" wide	3 strips, $2\frac{1}{2}$" wide	4 strips, $2\frac{1}{2}$" wide
	Piece 7b	5 strips, $2\frac{1}{2}$" wide	2 strips, $2\frac{1}{2}$" wide	4 strips, $2\frac{1}{2}$" wide

MAKE THE STRIP SETS

Information specific to the 9-block and 16-block quilts is given within brackets [ ].

1. Sew 5 strips of **fabric 8** to 4 strips of **fabric 9**, alternating them to make a strip set. Press the seam allowances toward **fabric 9**. Make 5 strip sets for the 25-block quilt [2 for the 9-block quilt, 3 for the 16-block quilt].

2. Cut the strip sets into $1\frac{1}{2}$" segments. You'll need 125 [45, 80] segments.

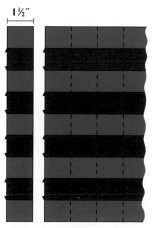

Cut segments from strip set.

3. Repeat Step 1 to sew 4 strips of **fabric 8** and 5 strips of **fabric 9** to make a strip set as shown. Press the seam allowances toward **fabric 9**. Make 4 [2, 3] strip sets. Cut the strip sets into $1\frac{1}{2}$" segments. You'll need 100 [36, 64] segments.

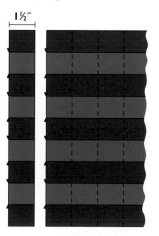

Cut segments from strip set.

4. Arrange 5 segments from Step 2 and 4 segments from Step 3 to make a checkerboard. You should have a **fabric 8** square in each corner. If all the seam allowances are pressed toward **fabric 9** and your $\frac{1}{4}$" seam allowances are consistent, the checkerboard segments should nest together perfectly at the opposing seams. If they don't, make any adjustments necessary so that the seams match. Sew the segments together. Press the seam allowances open. Make 25 [9, 16] checkerboard units.

5. Cut each strip of **fabric 10** and **11** into 3 equal lengths (approximately 14") and sew a **strip 10** to a **strip 11**. Press the seam toward the **strip 11**. Cut the strip set in half and sew the 2 halves together side by side. Cut four $1\frac{1}{2}$" wide segments from the strip set and arrange the segments to create a checkerboard. **Fabric 10** should be in the upper left corner.

6. Sew the segments together and press the seams open. Repeat to make 25 [9, 16] of these checkerboard units. Set them aside. Save any of the trimmings from the strip sets to use later if needed.

Fabric 10–11 checkerboard

Save Those Strips

Save extra pieces of your strip sets for use in the border or another project.

MAKE THE TEMPLATES

1. To make freezer-paper templates, trace your block drawing from the Master Cutting Guide onto freezer paper. You can also make cardboard or plastic templates using the methods described on pages 17–18. No matter which template material you choose, keep the following pieces together as 1 template. These will be used to cut pieces from the checkerboards.

- 8–9 checkerboard unit
- 10–11 checkerboard unit

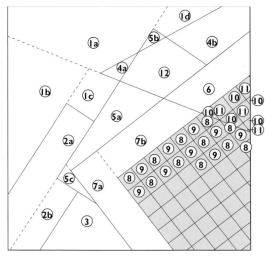

Cut one template for 8–9 checkerboard unit and one template for 10–11 checkerboard unit.

2. If you are using freezer-paper templates, make notations at each edge of each template indicating the amount of extra fabric to add when cutting—¼" for seam allowances on inside edges. Make sure each area on the freezer paper is marked with the number of the fabric to be cut.

CUT THE BLOCK PIECES

For cardboard or plastic templates, trace around them as described on pages 17–18.

1. For the **8–9 checkerboard area**, press the freezer-paper template on top of the checkerboard unit as shown. There should be ¼" of the pieced checkerboard showing at the top and left edges of the template. Cut out the piece with the edge of your ruler placed ¼" beyond the short upper right-hand edge. Place the ruler at the edge of the paper to cut the other 2 sides.

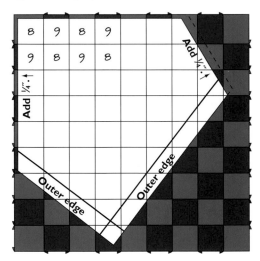

Iron freezer-paper template on checkerboard.

2. Repeat to make all the **8–9 checkerboard pieces** you need for your blocks.

3. Cut 25 [9, 16] of each of the remaining pieces with the templates except the **10–11 checkerboard section**. Do not cut the 10–11 checkerboard pieces from the template yet.

4. Stack the cut pieces in their proper relationship in a holding area of your table.

5. Now go back to the **10–11 checkerboard piece** you have set aside. This section will create an illusion of transparency, suggesting that a transparent color extends across the checkerboard, changing its color on a diagonal line as it crosses the **8–9 checkerboard**. Piecing 2 different color checkerboards together on the diagonal so that all the lines match up is tricky, but Special Lesson: Piecing Two different Checkerboards Together on a Diagonal Line in this chapter (page 73) makes the process a bit easier. Refer to those instructions now to piece the 2 checkerboards together so the seams match up and the transparency illusion is maintained. Then continue with Step 6.

6. Iron the freezer-paper template onto the **10–11 checkerboard piece**, aligning the edge of the template with the seamline you just sewed. Trim along the outside edge of the template. You may need to use some of the 10–11 trimmings to extend the checkerboard a bit along the outer edge.

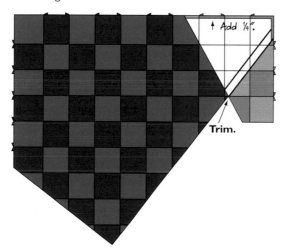

Iron template on small checkerboard and trim.

CONSTRUCT THE BLOCKS

1. Sew **pieces 7b** and **6** together at the diagonal seam and press the seam open.

2. Add the unit from Step 1 to the checkerboard unit. It is essential that the 2 diagonal seams match as you do so. Pin the points that need to maintain the illusion of transparency. Press the seam toward the **7b-6** combination piece.

3. Add piece **7a** to the left edge of the checkerboard and **7b** unit. Press the seam toward **7a** and set aside.

4. Sew **piece 5b** to **piece 1d**. Press the seam toward **piece 5b**.

5. Now sew **piece 5a** to **12** and add **4b**. Press the seams open. Add the **5b–1d unit** to the top. Take care to match the seams in these 2 pieces.

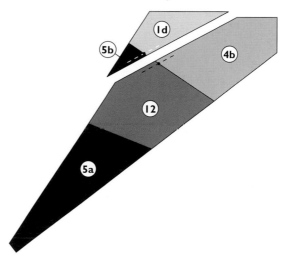

Match seams in both pieces.

6. Add the unit from Step 5 to the checkerboard unit from Step 3, again making sure the diagonal seams match and appear to continue as 1 line.

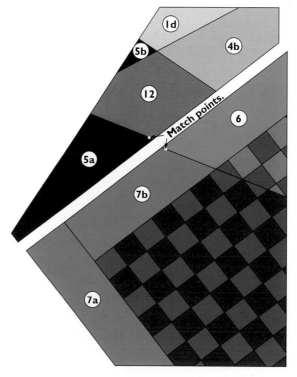

Match seams.

7. Sew **piece 2b** to **piece 3**. Press the seam toward **piece 2b**. Add **piece 5c** to the top edge of the unit and press toward **5c**. Add this 3-piece unit to the **7a–5a** side of the unit made in Step 6.

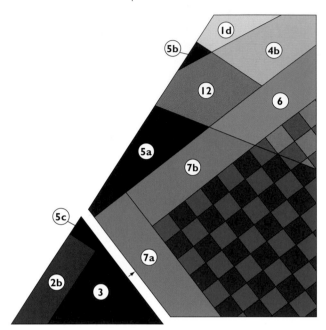

Combine pieces.

8. Sew **piece 1c** to **2a** and press the seam toward **piece 2a**. Add **piece 1b** to the side of this unit.

9. Add **piece 4a** to the short side of **piece 1a** and press toward **4**. Add this unit to the one made in Step 8.

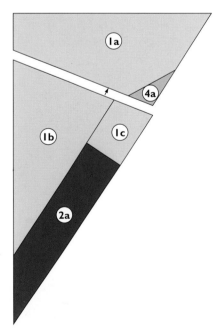

Combine pieces.

10. Clean up the edges of the 2 halves of the block by trimming a continuous straight line on each piece where the final seam will be. Be careful to remove as little fabric as possible in this process. Sew the 2 halves of the block together, making sure the seams on each edge of **piece 4a** match those of **piece 12**.

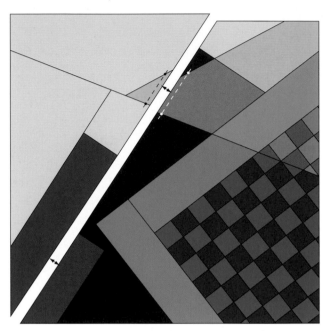

Match pieces.

SQUARE THE BLOCKS

Now that your blocks are pieced, it's important to trim them all to exactly 15″ square. The ½″ extra you added to all the outside edge pieces will ensure that you can cut a full 15″ block. (See the instructions on page 24 to square up your blocks using tape on the 15″ square ruler as a reference.)

If the taped references on the ruler don't match all the blocks exactly the same way, choose 1 or 2 references to match in all the blocks. Then trim the blocks around the edge of the 15″ ruler using 1 consistent reference point.

Piecing Two Different Checkerboards Together on a Diagonal Line

The 2 checkerboard pieces from the Advanced block are used to demonstrate this technique.

1. Place the 10–11 checkerboard on your worktable so that color 10 (green in my example) is in the upper left-hand corner of the piece.

2. Place the 8–9 checkerboard on top of the 10–11 checkerboard so that the short diagonal cut edge overlaps the left edge of the small checkerboard as shown. Align both the vertical and horizontal seams in the 2 pieces and make sure color 8 and color 10 share the same squares and color 9 and color 11 share the same squares.

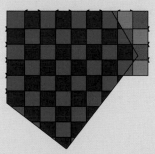

Overlap checkerboards and align seams.

3. Keep the 2 checkerboard pieces positioned this way without moving them. Place your cutting ruler so that the ½" line of the ruler is aligned with the cut edge of the 8–9 checkerboard as shown.

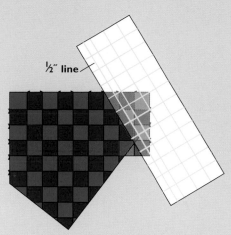

½" line

Place ruler ½" line on cut edge of 8–9 checkerboard.

4. Put the weight of the heel of your hand on the far side of the ruler so the cutting edge lifts up a little bit, and gently pull the 8–9 checkerboard piece out from under the ruler. The cutting edge of the ruler is now positioned correctly to cut the diagonal angle of piece 10–11. Make the cut. You may need to rotate the cutting mat so the ruler is to your left (if you are right-handed); be very careful not to disturb the position of the checkerboard or the ruler.

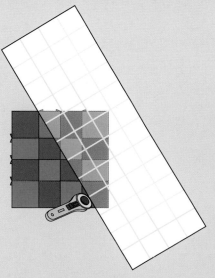

Cut edge of piece 10–11.

5. Place the 2 checkerboards right sides together, aligning the cut edges. Pin the seam carefully. Put a pin through every place the seams intersect along the ¼" seamline and check to make sure a pin intersects the seams correctly at the new seamline on the checkerboard piece on the bottom.

Pin seams at new seamline.

6. Machine baste a scant ¼" seam and check to see if the checkerboard seams match. If they don't, it will be easier to rip out and adjust a basted seam than a sewn seam. Make any necessary adjustments. If the seams do match, stitch over the basting with a normal-length stitch. Press the seam open.

AUDITION THE BLOCKS AS A QUILT

I always recommend looking at different ways to position or use the blocks before you decide to trim them to make a shifted image. Try the blocks in several different side-by-side settings, photographing each as you try it.

Option 1

Option 2

Option 3

Finally, check the blocks as a shifted image by using one of the diagrams on pages 26–29. I used the diagram on page 29 for trimming the 25 blocks from 15″ to 9″. Fold under the parts to be trimmed and put them up on your design wall, edge to edge, according to the diagram. Photograph this version as well.

Study the group of photos and decide which you like best. If you like the trimmed (folded under) version best, continue with Trim the Blocks for a Shifted Image below. If you prefer to use them as they are, go to Sew the Blocks Together.

TRIM THE BLOCKS FOR A SHIFTED IMAGE

For a shifted-image quilt, see The Shifted Image starting on page 29. Label and trim the blocks according to the diagram and trimming instructions.

SEW THE BLOCKS TOGETHER

Sew each row of blocks together. Press the seam allowances in opposite directions from row to row. When you sew the rows together, the seams will butt up against each other and the seams will match nicely. I like to press the row seams open to distribute the bulk.

MAKE THE BORDERS

See the section on borders on pages 31–33 to get ideas for bordering your quilt. Choose from one of the options there, design your own border, or complete your quilt with a border similar to the one in the quilt photo on page 66, made from the trimmings that remained after cutting the 15″ blocks into 9″ blocks.

VARIATIONS ON A THEME

So far, all the Multi-View Image quilts presented have been square quilts made from square, pieced blocks. There are, however, many other possible variations when making these quilts. The possibilities include quilts from rectangular blocks, rectangular quilts from square blocks, quilts made from blocks that change entirely from corner to corner when shifted, quilts made with techniques other than piecing, traditional quilt blocks trimmed for a shifted image, and quilts made from blocks with changing color or fabric instead of identical blocks.

Quilts From Rectangular Blocks

You can make Multi-View Image quilts using rectangular blocks. Here is a simple variation of the traditional Moon Over the Mountain block designed as a 12″ × 18″ rectangle.

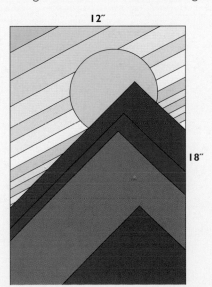

12″

18″

Rectangular block

Here is the result of using this rectangular block to create a shifted-image quilt.

Moon Over Mountains, 45″ × 56″, by Lorraine Torrence, 2005

This is one of my rectangular quilts made from square blocks. The trimming diagram on page 88 can be used for this quilt.

Mimosa Sunrise, 60˝ × 45˝, designed by Lorraine Torrence, pieced by Diane Roubal and Lorraine Torrence, quilted by Lisa Taylor, 2005

Quilts That Change Entirely From Corner to Corner

To design a quilt in which the upper corner blocks both change to completely different blocks in the lower corners, you must design a block whose corners are all different. Then you must trim it down to a cut size no larger than one-fourth of the total size of the original block (half the width and half the height).

The 36-block quilt on page 80, *Studio Corners,* almost achieves this goal but maintains a little bit of the white fabric in every block. The rectangular quilt *Mimosa Sunrise* above also comes close to achieving this complete transition since we trimmed a 15˝ block to 7½˝. But at least a little of the gray batik fabric with spirals appears in every block. Eileen Alber's quilt *Marimeko Swatches* on page 79 achieves this change beautifully.

Quilts Made With Other Techniques

It might be hard to get an appliqué quilter to cut up hand-appliquéd blocks, but appliquéd blocks—or blocks made with any technique, for that matter—can be trimmed and shifted just as pieced blocks can be trimmed and shifted. For purposes of the shifted-image effect, the technique is less important than the design of the block. You will still need to make opposite corners different and create areas of varying scale and value to make the shift effective. Try the shifted-image approach with fused appliqué blocks; stenciled, stamped, airbrushed, or silk-screened blocks; manipulated fabric blocks; or any technique that interests you.

Multi-View Image Quilts Made From Traditional Quilt Blocks

Traditional pieced blocks are also perfectly good candidates for shifted-image quilts. Here is a traditional Ohio Star block design.

The trick, of course, is to use different colors of fabrics in opposite corners.

Traditional Ohio Star block with different colors in opposite corners

The 16 Ohio Star blocks make an interesting quilt when trimmed for a shifted image, set on point, and bordered with the block trimmings.

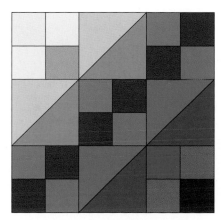

Block design for Jacob's Ladder quilt

Shifted Ohio Star, 54″ × 54″, designed by Lorraine Torrence, pieced by Lorraine Torrence and Cindy Hayes, quilted by Diane Roubal, 2005

A Jacob's Ladder block done as a Multi-View Image quilt could look like this.

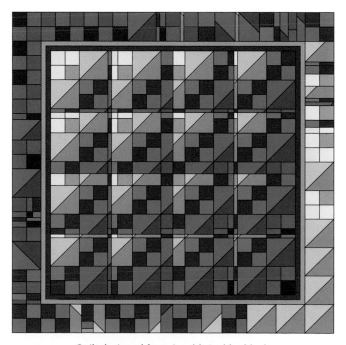

Quilt designed from Jacob's Ladder block

Quilts Made With Blocks Whose Color Changes as the Image Shifts

What if the position of the pieces in the cut block were not the only thing that changed among the blocks as they shifted across the quilt top? A group of blocks whose color changes as well as shifts is intriguing. You can achieve this color change by using a fabric that changes in color from selvage to selvage, a gradation of hand-dyed fabrics, or even a carefully selected range of solid colors. Select a noticeable shape and cut each piece for this shape in a different value or color for each block.

Thunderclouds Approaching, on page 4, contains a changing hand-dyed fabric by Judy Robertson in the large area of each block.

Another example might look like the quilt to the right.

Moon Over Mountains **with different colored moons in each block**

The variations possible with this technique are limitless. I'm sure you will be able to think of possibilities that I have not even imagined!

GALLERY

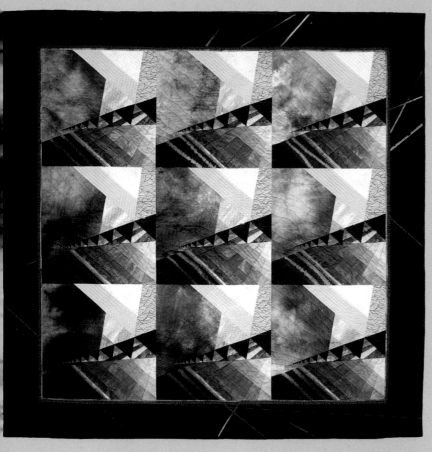

La Conner 9-Block, 73 $\frac{1}{2}$″ × 74″, designed by Lorraine Torrence, pieced by Lorraine Torrence and Cory Volkert, 2003

This quilt is made of 9 untrimmed 20″ blocks. Originally I planned this quilt as a 25-block Multi-View Image quilt. Instead, I decided to make two quilts: one a 9-block quilt without trimming the blocks and shifting the image (this one), and the other a 16-block shifted-image quilt (see *Thunderclouds Approaching* on page 4).

Marimeko Swatches, 46″ × 44″, by Eileen Alber, 2005

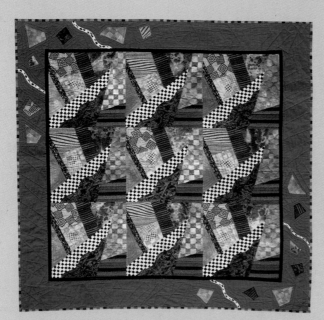

Checkerboards, 55″ × 54″, by Eileen Alber, 2005

Eileen decided to leave these 9 blocks untrimmed. With no trimmings to use, she designed a border that repeats the wavy lines and floating shapes suggested in the quilt blocks.

Eileen felt the quilt was too busy with the blocks touching each other so she added sashing to calm it down. Her choice makes a more successful quilt—wouldn't you agree?

Studio Corners, 45″ × 47 1/2″,
designed by Lorraine Torrence,
pieced by Cindy Hayes,
quilted by Gretchen Engle, 2005

This design was generated as I looked through the tipped Multi-View lens at the corner of my studio. I simplified the image, took some liberties with the color, and repeated the image 36 times. Trimming the block to one-fourth its original size made the image change almost entirely from one corner to the opposite, except for the small amount of white that remains in the upper left block.

Pick Up Sticks, 62″ × 62″, by Cory Volkert, 2005

Cory trimmed her blocks for a shifted image but chose to border the quilt with three pieces of the fabric used in her blocks rather than employ her block trimmings. The narrow red inner border helps contain the quilt and repeats the similar red line that is part of the block design.

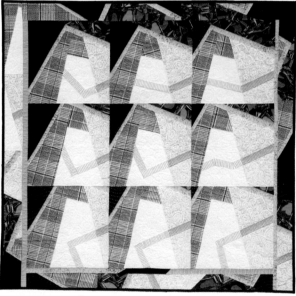

Groov'n, 41 1/2″ × 41″, by Mary Ann Musgrove, 1999

After completing her quilt top, Mary Ann thought the large white area was too empty. She solved the problem by stitching a continuation of the green stripe. Her ghostly repetition is a satin-stitched stripe that doubles as quilting as it goes through all layers. She made her stitched stripe continuation even more lively by letting it change and dance around as it moves from block to block. From the collection of Bud and Lynn Moore.

M/V Cutting Edges 9-Block,
40½″ × 41″,
**by Lorraine Torrence,
quilted by Gretchen Engle, 2005**

This design is easy and
effective as a trimmed block
repeat. I have used it several
times with different colors
and fabrics.

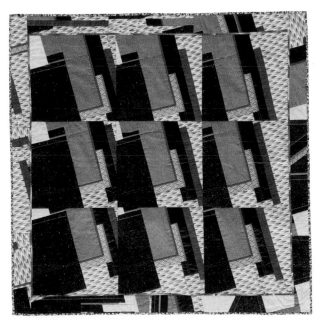

Surely You Quilt, 40″ × 40″, **by Susan Pelton, 1995**

Susan made this quilt in my Multi-View Images class,
her very first quilt class. Since her mother was a quilter,
everyone assumed she was a quilter too. The title of
her quilt reflects this assumption. As an accomplished
sewer, Susan had no trouble with technique and was
able to manage the even, though very narrow, strips
easily. (See Special Lesson: Sewing Very Even ¼″
Strips on page 51 for a reminder on how to sew them.)

Mother Earth, Father Sun, 71″ × 71″, **by Cory Volkert, 2005**

Cory used her block trimmings to intensify the
sun and earth corners of the quilt. Keeping the
trimmings the same size as the block width also
enhances the sense of rhythm produced by the
repeated sun and earth images.

Pinwheels and Checkerboards,
66″ × 66″,
designed by Lorraine Torrence,
pieced by Cindy Hayes,
quilted by Kate Sullivan, 2005

One of the untrimmed arrangements of the Easy block project on page 44 was interesting enough that I made a second quilt consisting of 16 untrimmed blocks in different colors.

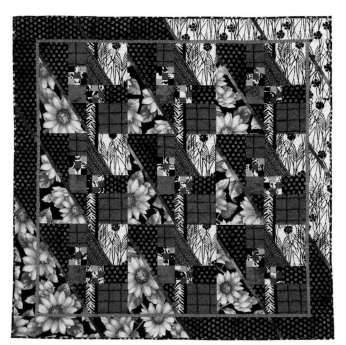

Sunflowers, **54″ × 54″, by Cory Volkert, 2005**

The strong graphic quality of Cory's block design did not benefit from trimming, so she left the blocks untrimmed. The border was made from extra fabric since there were no trimmings to use.

Multi-View Staircase, **41″ × 41″, by Lynn Koolish, 2001**

This quilt was inspired by the view of an open concrete staircase. This strong graphic design clearly shows the image shift as sections grow and diminish. The trimmings balance the color nicely and seem to provide a plane above which the 9-block interior appears to float.

APPENDIX

Calculating Yardage

Once you have designed your block and have decided on the number and original size of the blocks, you are ready to figure the yardage requirements.

PIECES CUT FROM ONE FABRIC

If you are using the Tape-on-the-Ruler method, use the measurements of the pieces. Remember to add seam allowances to the dimensions of the pieces you drew on the Master Cutting Guide. Determine the width of strip you will start with, then how many pieces you can cut from a 40″ width of fabric. From this, calculate how many strips you will need and the resulting yardage.

If you are using templates, lay out the template on any piece of fabric in the width you are likely to buy to determine how many pieces you can get across the width. For example, let's say your template is about 10″ × 11″. You can fit 4 templates across the fabric width if you alternate and dovetail them. For a 9-block quilt, you need 3 rows, each 12″ × 42″, to cut these 9 pieces (2 rows of 4 template pieces plus a third row to cut the ninth piece). Three rows of 12″ comes to exactly 1 yard, but I recommend increasing the yardage to purchase at least 1¼ yards—more if you think you might want to use this fabric in the border. If your fabric is directional, all the templates will need to face the same direction and you will need additional fabric.

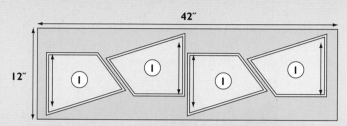

Dovetail templates across the width of the fabric when possible.

PIECES CUT FROM STRIP SETS

For straight checkerboards and strips, use the measurements of the strips and the number of strips needed to figure the yardage.

When cutting irregular shapes with templates or the Tape-on-the-Ruler cutting method, you will need to determine how many pieces you can cut from each strip set and thus how many of each strip set you will need.

As an example, let's say your strip set is made up of 8 strips. Draw a sketch representing this strip set to help you keep track of fabrics and dimensions. It's helpful to include the cut dimensions of each strip. Generally strips are cut across the width of the fabric, so we will assume each is 42″ long.

Measure the size of the piece that will be cut from the strip set and sketch it positioned on the strip set as you would cut the pieces from it. How many of these pieces can you fit on the strip set? If the piece is 7″ wide, you can fit 5 across the strip set. If you need 9 pieces, then you will need 2 strip sets. Double the width of each strip to determine the inches needed; divide by 36 to calculate yardage. Round up to the nearest eighth yard. If any strips are cut from the same fabric, add all the widths together to get total inches before dividing by 36 for the yardage.

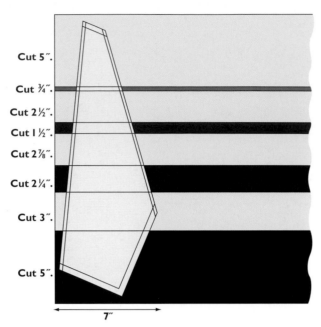

Cut 5″.
Cut ¾″.
Cut 2½″.
Cut 1½″.
Cut 2⅞″.
Cut 2¼″.
Cut 3″.
Cut 5″.

7″

Determine how many pieces can be cut from one strip set.

It is always a good idea to purchase more of each fabric than your final calculation in order to account for shrinkage, changing your mind, errors, and using the fabric in the border. Even if you use the trimmings of the blocks as part of the border, you may need to quiet down or simplify the border by using a larger amount of one of the fabrics from your block.

The Formula for Designing Any Shift

SQUARE BLOCKS

The four cutting diagrams on pages 26–29 are certainly not the only options for shifting images in a Multi-View Image quilt. You may want to start with a larger block, trim the block to a smaller size, use a different number of blocks in each row, or cut each block using a larger amount of shift. In this section I'll provide a formula that will help you come up with your own cutting scenario if one of the four I have given you does not fit the bill.

Let's say that O is the size of the **original** block, T is the size of the **trimmed** block, n is the **number** of blocks in the row, and S is the amount in inches you **shift** the

position of the cut block from the starting position in the upper left corner of the upper left block. To work the formula, you have to know 3 of the 4 variables.

O = Original block size

T = Trimmed block size

n = Number of blocks in a row

S = Shift (in inches)

$$\frac{(O - T)}{(n - 1)} = S$$

Now, before you panic and say you never were good at algebra in high school, take a deep breath; let's go through the formula so you will understand it.

The first part of the equation is (O – T). This is the difference between the size of the original block and the trimmed block. You have to determine this first and then continue with the equation. Let's say you start with a 15″ original block (like all the original blocks in the four quilt projects). Let us also assume that you will trim all the blocks to 12″. The difference between these two numbers is 3″. That is the number that will replace the (O – T) part of the equation.

Now let's look at the next part: (n – 1). This means that you are looking for the number of blocks in a row **less one.** Why? Because if there are 3 blocks in a row, for example, you will shift the cut twice. The position of the first cut block is always in the upper left corner of the upper left block. You move the position once for the second block and once again for the third block. You will move (shift) the block twice. So the number you get for the second part of the equation in this example is 2. Now you have a fraction:

$3″/2$

This means that the 3″ difference has to be divided by 2 to get the part of the shift you will cut each time you move to the next block. So the shift is 1½″. This scenario is illustrated in our first diagram on page 26. In the first block, you cut 3″ off 2 sides. Remember that the top and bottom cuts remain the same across the rows. In the second block, you cut 1½″ off each of the 2 sides, and in the third block, you cut 3″ off 1 side. You can test the formula for each of the diagrams in The Shifted Image, beginning on page 26.

Now, what if you decide you want a trimmed 12″ block and a 16-block quilt (4 blocks across and 4 down), and you want to be able to shift the block 1½″ each time? This amount of shift is what I have determined to be the minimum amount that will have a noticeable impact on the design in a quilt of this size. Now the unknown quantity is the size of the original block. Our equation will look like this:

$$\frac{(O - 12″)}{(4 - 1)} = 1½″$$

The (4 – 1) part you can change to 3:

$$\frac{(O - 12″)}{3} = 1½″$$

To find the value of O, first multiply the 1½″ by the 3. That gives us 4½″. Our new equation is:

O – 12″ = 4½″

In other words, **something** minus 12 equals 4½. Add 4½″ to 12 and you get the answer: O is 16½″. A cutting diagram for this situation is found on page 28.

You can calculate any scenario this way and draw a cutting diagram for yourself to make the trimming easy to follow. Notice that the cutting diagrams show that all the blocks in each vertical row have the same amount cut off the left and right sides of the blocks in that row. The only difference is the position of the horizontal cuts as the block moves down. Similarly, the blocks in each horizontal row have the same amount cut off the top and bottom edges. So the position of the cut block in relation to the original block is a combination of the vertical and horizontal positions. Study the cutting diagrams to understand the principal of the shifting image before you make your own diagram.

RECTANGULAR BLOCKS

There is nothing mysterious about making and trimming multiple rectangular blocks. The difference is that you will have to use the formula **twice**, once for the width and once for the height. Up to this point, the amount of shift has been the same in both the horizontal rows and the vertical rows. When you use a rectangular block, the O quantity, or the size of the original block, is different in the horizontal rows and the vertical rows. In a rectangular block the O quantity represents the **width** of the block in the horizontal rows and the **height** of the block in the vertical rows. You will have to use the formula twice to determine either the amount of the shift, the size of the cut block (height or width), or the number of blocks in the rows (vertically and horizontally). The rule of thumb is this: *Any time the quantity of any variable is different in the horizontal row from the vertical row, the formula must be worked twice.*

As an example, the rectangular block from *Moon Over Mountains* (see page 75) measures 12″ wide × 18″ high. As before, you have to know three of the variables to determine the fourth. In this case you already know the size of the original block. This is the O quantity. It is 12″ when you use the formula for the horizontal rows and 18″ when you use the formula for the vertical rows. The other variables include the size of the cut block, the number of blocks in the rows, and the amount of the shift in inches.

Are there any of these variables that you have decided upon at the outset? Let's say you want 16 blocks in the quilt: 4 across in the horizontal rows and 4 down in the vertical rows. Now the n (number of blocks in a row) quantity is established. It is 4 in the horizontal direction and 4 in the vertical direction. Of the other two variables, size of cut block and amount of shift, which do you want to decide in advance? How about the size of the cut block? Let's say you want the size of the cut block to be 9″ × 12″. Now you know the T quantity: it is 9″ in the horizontal rows and 12″ in the vertical rows. Now you can use the formula to determine the amount of shift both vertically and horizontally.

For the horizontal rows:

$$\frac{(O - T)}{(n - 1)} = S \quad \text{or} \quad \frac{(12″ - 9″)}{(4 - 1)} = S \quad \text{or} \quad \frac{3″}{3} = 1″ \text{ shift}$$

For the vertical rows:

$$\frac{(O - T)}{(n - 1)} = S \quad \text{or} \quad \frac{(18″ - 12″)}{(4 - 1)} = S \quad \text{or} \quad \frac{6″}{3} = 2″ \text{ shift}$$

A cutting diagram for this scenario would look like the one shown on the next page.

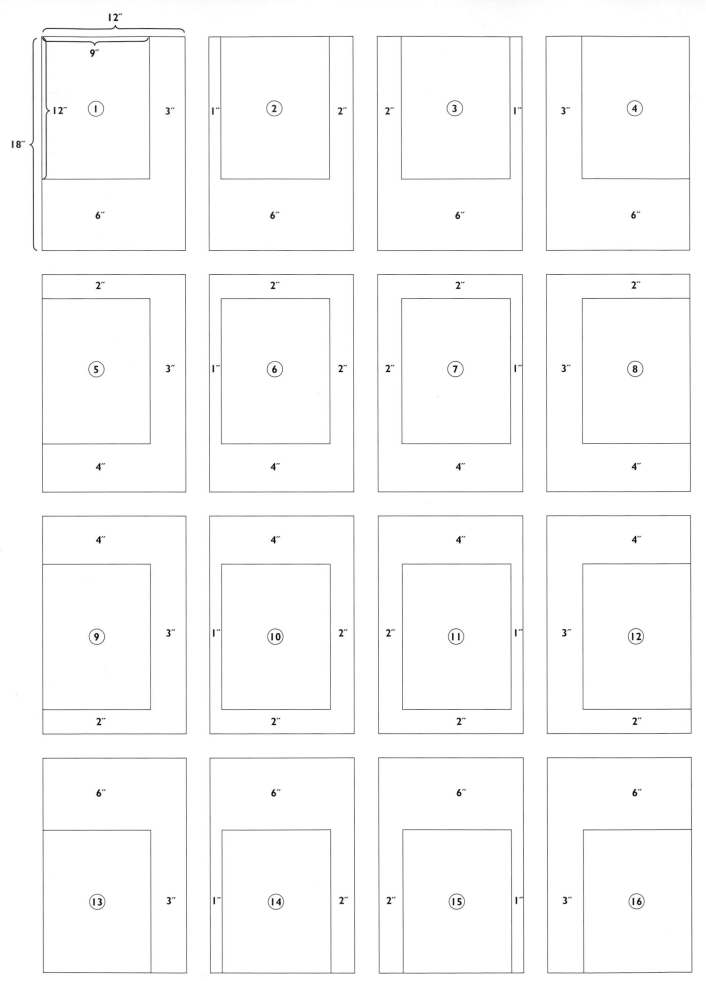

Cutting diagram for a rectangular quilt from rectangular blocks

RECTANGULAR QUILTS FROM SQUARE BLOCKS

Making a rectangular quilt from a square block is simply a matter of making the number of blocks in a row different from the number of rows.

Let's start with a 15″ × 15″ block and assume you want the size of the trimmed blocks to remain square at 12″ × 12″. But you want the number of blocks to be 5 across in the horizontal rows and 7 down in the vertical rows. Since the quantity of the n value is different in the horizontal row from the vertical row, you know you have to work the formula twice. You will be looking for the amount of shift (S) in the horizontal rows and in the vertical rows.

Your formula will look like this for the horizontal rows:

$$\frac{(O - T)}{(n - 1)} = S \qquad \frac{(15″ - 12″)}{(5 - 1)} = S \qquad \frac{3″}{4} = \tfrac{3}{4}″ \text{ shift}$$

For the vertical rows, it looks like this:

$$\frac{(O - T)}{(n - 1)} = S \qquad \frac{(15″ - 12″)}{(7 - 1)} = S \qquad \frac{3″}{6} = \tfrac{1}{2}″ \text{ shift}$$

This was a surprise to me! I know that a ¾″ shift or a ½″ shift is hardly noticeable in a shifted-image quilt. I use 1½″ as the minimum amount of shift in a block that is cut down to 12″. So let's work the formula again and look for the size of the original block (O) instead of the amount of shift (S). For the horizontal rows our formula now looks like this:

$$\frac{(O - T)}{(n - 1)} = S \qquad \frac{(O - 12″)}{(5 - 1)} = 1\tfrac{1}{2}″ \qquad \frac{(O - 12″)}{4} = 1\tfrac{1}{2}″$$

You have to multiply the 1½″ by the 4 to come up with the solution to the (O – 12″) part of the equation, which is 6″. If the difference between O and 12″ is 6″, then you know that O = 18″. So the size of your original block has to be 18″.

But now I am thinking that blocks cut down to 12″ will produce a quilt that is about 72″ wide and 96″ long with borders added. Hmmm. That's bigger than I want. Back to the drawing board!

If I use a 15″ original block size, what size would I have to cut the blocks to in order to produce a quilt in the size range I want? My final solution was to cut the 15″ block down to 7½″, and make the quilt 5 blocks across and 7 blocks down. After sewing 7½″ square blocks, the center of the quilt will measure 35″ × 49″ (after seam allowances are subtracted). Adding another 6″ to 8″ on each side for borders gives me approximately the size quilt I want. See the cutting diagram for this quilt on page 88. You can also use the cutting diagram sideways for a horizontal quilt.

Tape-on-the-Ruler Cutting

Here are some additional step-by-step instructions to practice cutting using the Tape-on-the-Ruler technique. These directions are a continuation of cutting for the sample block shown. See pages 19–20 for cutting piece 1. Now we'll use the same methods to cut the rest of the pieces of the block.

Looking at piece 3a, you'll see that it also has an outside edge and right-angle corner, but this piece has 5 sides instead of 4. First decide on the direction of the grainline and draw those arrows on the Master Cutting Guide in the 3a area. Again, I recommend placing the straight of grain on the 2 outside edges for the stability of the block unless there is a visual reason to do otherwise.

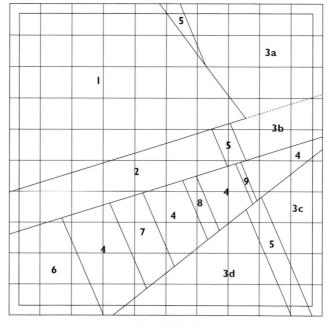

Sample block

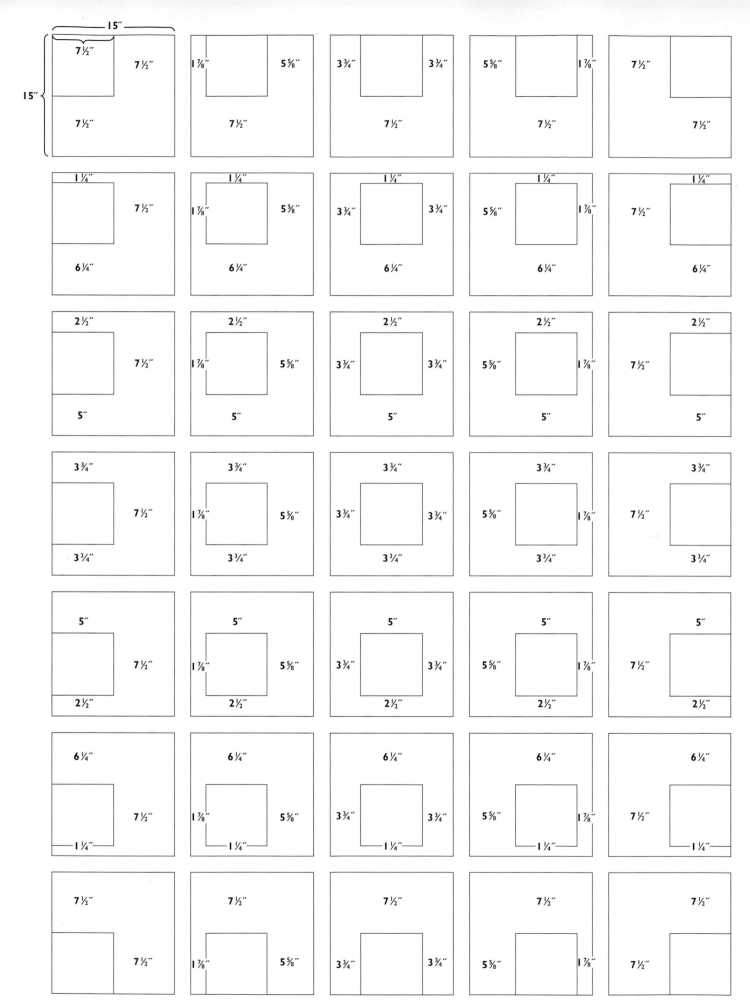

Cutting diagram for a rectangular quilt from square blocks

(Continued from page 87.)

1. Measure piece 3a vertically from the added ½″ line at the top edge down to a seam allowance below the lowest point in the shape. The measurement is 6¼″. Cut a strip that is ¼″ wider, about 6½″ wide, across the width of fabric 3. Cut off the selvage on the right end with a cut that is perpendicular to the long edge of the strip. This right angle will become the top right-hand corner of piece 3a.

2. Your next cut should be the one that is most parallel to the edge of the strip you just cut (the right-angle cut at the end of the strip). On this piece, that cut will be the C–D line. This will separate the "chunk" from the strip. (The fabric is shown superimposed over the Master Cutting Guide for illustration purposes only.)

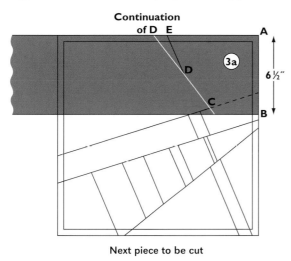

Next piece to be cut

3. Identify the cutting edge of your ruler and place it on the C–D line on the Master Cutting Guide. Position your ruler so that the ¼″ line on the ruler is on top of the C–D line. Now tape the existing reference point at the right-angle corner. This corresponds to the right-angle cut you made on your strip of fabric. Place 2 pieces of ½″ removable tape on the ruler along the ½″ line and note "CUT EDGE" on the tape.

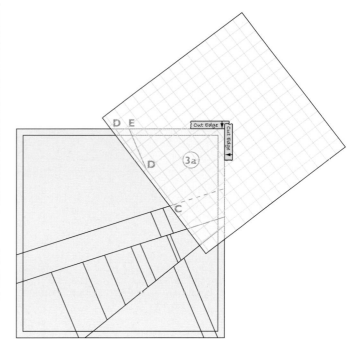

Tape references on ruler.

4. Move the taped ruler from the Master Cutting Guide to the fabric strip for piece 3a on your cutting mat. Align the taped angle with the upper right corner of the strip. Now you can cut across the strip along the cutting edge of the ruler. Cut all the way across the strip; you will cut the D–E edge later. Remove the tape from the ruler. Note: If you are right-handed, you will need to rotate your cutting mat or walk around your cutting table to actually make the cut.

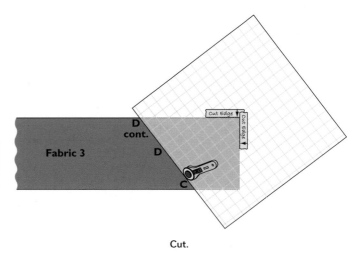

Cut.

5. Two more cuts are needed to finish this piece. It doesn't matter which you do first. Let's do the B–C line next. Notice that on the Master Cutting Guide, this is a dotted line. This means that 2 pieces of the same fabric are sewn together here. The seam is not a visual division but one to make the block construction easier. For cutting purposes, you treat it like a solid line. Place the cutting edge of your ruler on that line and then move it to align the ¼" line of your ruler directly on the B–C line. Now tape the existing reference points—the right angle at the top right-hand corner as well as the C–D edge. Tape on the outside of the corner with the ½" removable tape and on the outside of the C–D line with the ¼" masking tape. Mark the ½" tape with arrows pointing to the "CUT EDGE" sides.

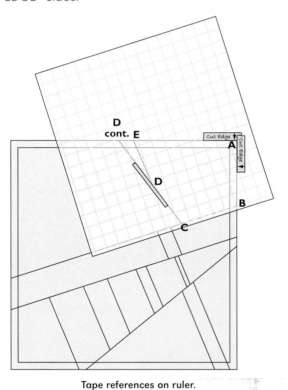

Tape references on ruler.

6. Move the taped ruler from the Master Cutting Guide to the cutting mat. Position the fabric piece under the ruler with the taped references aligned with their counterparts on the fabric piece. Cut the B–C edge and remove the tape from the ruler.

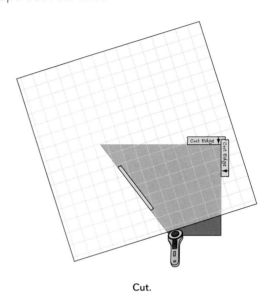

Cut.

7. The final side to cut on piece 3a is the D–E edge. Place the cutting edge of the ruler ¼" beyond the D–E line on the Master Cutting Guide. Tape the existing reference points as you have done before: ½" removable tape around the outside corner and ¼" masking tape beyond the seamlines that you have already cut. Mark the tape with arrows indicating the "CUT EDGE" sides.

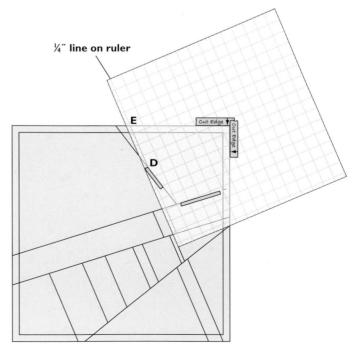

Tape references on ruler.

8. Cut the D–E line and remove the tape from the ruler.

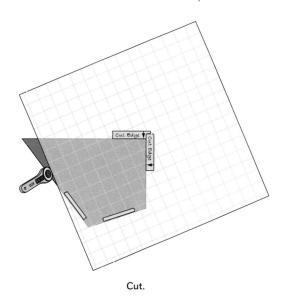

Cut.

CUTTING A COMBINATION PIECE

Combination pieces are pieces made up of more than 1 fabric. It can be 2 or more strips of any width sewn together into a unit or strip set. Any time you can cut a **combination piece,** do it! Accuracy is improved when you sew before you cut rather than cutting before you sew. Make strip sets of 2 or more pieces of fabric if the seamlines are all parallel. There are 3 such areas in the sample block. In the illustration below, they are shown in blue, red, and green.

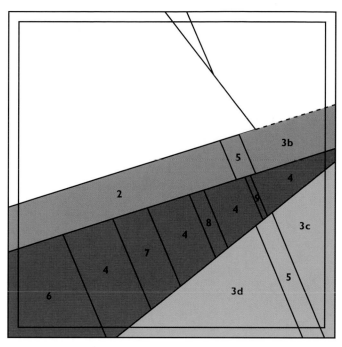

Three strip-pieced (combination) areas

1. Begin with the blue section. Measure each piece of fabric at its widest point, **perpendicular to the seamlines** in the area. Make sure you add seam allowances to all interior seams. The fabric 2 piece is 12″ wide, including a ¼″ seam allowance on the inner edge and the ½″ outside edge allowance that already exists on the Master Cutting Guide. Write down the width of the piece on the Master Cutting Guide.

2. Piece 5 in this area is 1½″ wide, including the seam allowances on either side. Record this measurement on the Master Cutting Guide. Piece 3b is just over 5¼″ wide. Record this as 5½″ on the Master Cutting Guide. Cut 1 strip from each of the 3 fabrics in the widths you recorded. Sew them together with a ¼″ seam allowance and press the seams toward the center strip (fabric 5).

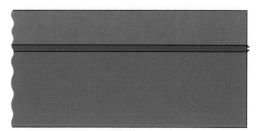

Strip set

3. Place the cutting edge of the ruler on the Master Cutting Guide ¼″ beyond the bottom edge of the combined piece and tape the existing reference points—the seamlines that are on both sides of the fabric 5 strip in the pieced strip set. Place tape on both of these lines and draw an arrow pointing to the side of each piece of tape that represents the seamline. Write "SEAM" on the tape.

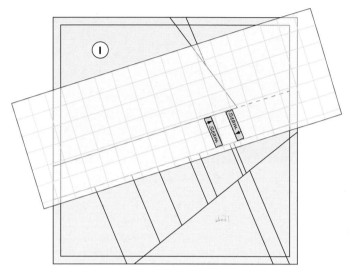

Tape references on ruler.

4. Move the taped ruler to the cutting mat on top of the strip set. Align the tape with the seamline and cut.

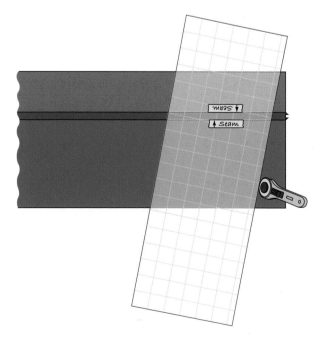

Position ruler and cut.

5. The 2 edges of this piece are parallel, so you can measure across the combined piece and add two ¼″ seam allowances to the measurement. The section is 2″ wide, and the addition of seam allowances make the segment 2½″. Cut a segment this wide starting from the edge of the strip set you just cut. You can repeat to cut as many segments as you need for the blocks.

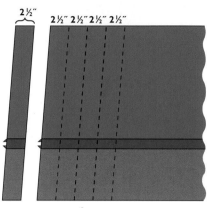

Cut 2½″ segments.

6. The red section can also be cut from a strip set because all the seamlines in this section are parallel. It is the fabric 6-4-7-4-8-4-9-4 series. Measure across each fabric strip **perpendicular** to the seamlines and add ¼″ seam allowances and the ½″ extra along the outside edge of the block. Write the cut measurements for each section on the Master Cutting Guide as an easy reminder of how wide to cut the strips of each fabric. There are times when you may not get all your pieces out of one strip set. Cut the strips, sew, and press. Make as many strip sets as you need to cut all your pieces.

7. Place the cutting edge of your ruler on your Master Cutting Guide ¼″ beyond the bottom edge of the 6-4-7-4-8-4-9-4 section. Mark the reference points with tape. In this case, the reference points will be the seamlines in the strip sets. You will not need to mark each one with tape; 1 or 2 will be enough. Identify the seam you are indicating (seam between fabric 7 and 4, for example) and draw arrows to the side of each piece of tape adjacent to the seam.

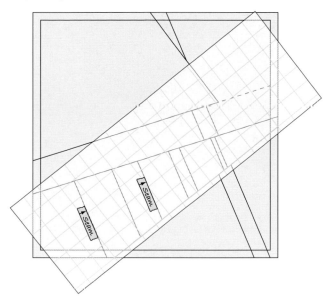

Tape references on ruler.

8. Move the ruler to the cutting mat on top of the strip set in the same orientation. Cut the first edge of the piece.

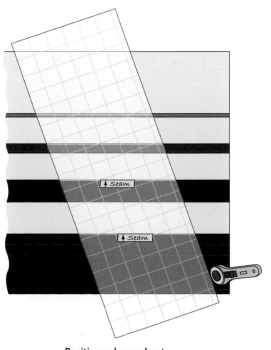

Position ruler and cut.

9. Now you can mark the references for the top edge of the piece. As before, place the ruler's cutting edge ¼″ beyond the top edge of the piece on the Master Cutting Guide and tape the reference points. You will now have the additional reference point of the edge you just cut. Mark this with ¼″ tape along the outside edge of the seamline and draw an arrow to the other side of the tape and label it "CUT EDGE." Remove the ruler from the Master Cutting Guide and place it on the cutting mat on top of the strip set with the cut end. Align all the taped references with their corresponding seams and cut edges. Cut the second edge.

10. The remaining section of the block, the green section, can be cut from a strip set made of 2 strips of fabric 3 and 1 strip of fabric 5 sewn between them. Again, determine the width of the strips to be cut for the strip set by measuring across the widest part of the area, **perpendicular** to the seamlines. Add ¼″ seam allowances on interior seams.

11. Record the measurements on the Master Cutting Guide. Sew the strips together and press the seams toward the center strip.

12. Place the cutting edge of the ruler ¼″ beyond the top edge of the green section on the Master Cutting Guide. Tape the seamline references and make notations on the tape.

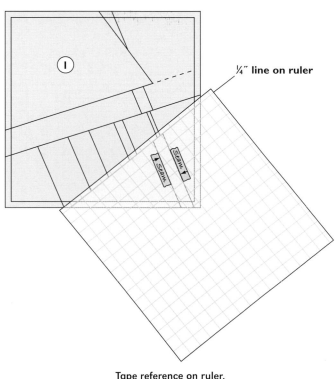

¼″ line on ruler

Tape reference on ruler.

13. Move the taped ruler to the cutting mat on top of the strip set at the top end. Align the tape with the seams of the strip set. Cut the top edge of the section.

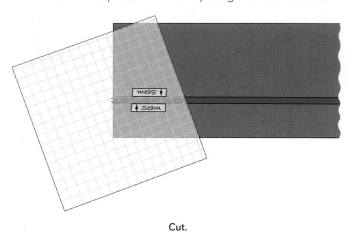

Cut.

14. Next you will cut the bottom right-hand corner of the green section. Place the corner of the 15″ square ruler along the line on the Master Cutting Guide that is ½″ outside the bottom right-hand edge. Tape the existing reference points with the ½″ tape (the seamlines) and ¼″ masking tape for the seam allowance at the top edge. Mark the tape with the appropriate notations. Place the ruler over the fabric strip set on the cutting mat. Align the tape with the reference points on the fabric piece and cut the right angle of the piece around the corner of the square ruler.

15. There is 1 remaining piece to add to the collection of pieces you have cut for the sample block. This is the small piece of fabric 5 along the top left edge of the 3a piece. The easiest way to deal with a piece like this is to cut a 1½″ × 6″ piece of fabric 5 and sew it to the D–E edge of piece 3a. Measure to obtain the dimension to cut. Press the seam and then trim piece 5 with cuts that continue the existing angles on the edges of piece 3a.

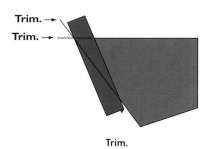

Trim.

16. Arrange all the cut pieces in their proper relationship in preparation for sewing them together.

ABOUT THE AUTHOR

Lorraine Torrence lives in Seattle, Washington, with her husband and near her two grown children and her grandsons. After earning a BFA and an MFA in sculpture, she stumbled into quilting and has enjoyed teaching (and constantly learning more about) this fabulous art form since 1972. Her first book, *Design Essentials: The Quilter's Guide*, was published in 1998.

She has two lines of wearable art patterns and can't seem to decide which she likes making more, quilts or garments—so she keeps doing both!

Visit Lorraine's website at www.lorrainetorrence.com.

INDEX

Great Titles
from C&T PUBLISHING

THINKING outside the BLOCK

Step by Step to Dynamic Quilts

Sandi Cummings with Karen Flamme

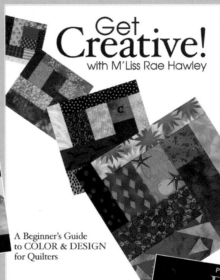

Get Creative!
with M'Liss Rae Hawley

A Beginner's Guide to COLOR & DESIGN for Quilters

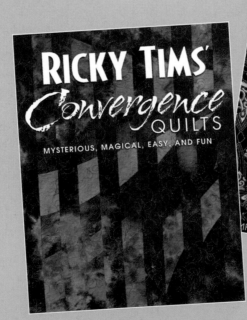

RICKY TIMS' Convergence QUILTS

MYSTERIOUS, MAGICAL, EASY, AND FUN

PAULA NADELSTERN
PUZZLE QUILTS

MPLE BLOCKS, COMPLEX FABRICS